JAPAN

JAPAN

Strategy of the Unseen

MICHEL RANDOM

Translated from the French by Cyprian P. Blamires

First published as
Japon: La stratégie de l'invisible
© 1985 by Editions du Félin — Michel
Random

First English edition 1987
English translation © Thorsons Publishing
Group Ltd 1987

British Library Cataloguing
in Publication Data

Random, Michel
Japan: the strategy of the unseen.
1. Japan—Civilization—1945-
I. Title   II. Japon. *English*
952.04'8   DS822.5

ISBN 1-85274-024-8

Crucible is an imprint of
The Aquarian Press, part of the
Thorsons Publishing Group,
Denington Estate, Wellingborough,
Northamptonshire, NN8 2RQ

Printed in Great Britain
by Woolnough Bookbinding,
Irthlingborough, Northamptonshire

CONTENTS

ACKNOWLEDGEMENTS

I would like to thank Eiji Hattori and Louis Frédéric for their kind suggestions and Miss Dominique Caillier for her close collaboration; also Pierre Belfond for permission to publish a few extracts from the preface to my book: *Le Traité des cinq anneaux de Miyamoto Musashi* (Editions Belfond).

A word of thanks too to all my Japanese friends, company directors, and martial arts teachers, to whom I am greatly indebted for showing me the subtle ways of the inner strategy of serenity.

INTRODUCTION

1. Japan: Paradoxes from another planet

Japan is a whole unknown continent. It is a strange mingling of old and new, a blend of hoary tradition with modern economic reality; a culture so remote from our own in the West that we have immense difficulty understanding it. But this is a culture we cannot afford to ignore in the modern world. This book aims to provide a key to the enigma of Japan.

Tradition and modern life can be kept apart in the West, but not in Japan. At the end of his busy day, the Japanese businessman goes home and exchanges his suit for a magnificent ornamental kimono; that is his way of unwinding. And the real inner essence of his existence resides in the traditional element in his life, his home, and his wife's attentive and kindly welcome: apart from this, all his activity amounts to little more than a procession of duties and obligations. One of my friends, the president of a large company, spends all his free time singing pieces from the *nō* theatre. Another is an enthusiast for the martial arts, while a third relaxes over a game of *go* with his friends.

This fusion of culture, tradition and economics, is the inspiration for my book. What I want to do is to show how to make sense of the two faces of Japanese reality; to demonstrate how to view these two faces as the two separate parts of one mind. Anyone who wants to understand contemporary Japan, and especially anyone who hopes to do business there or collaborate with the Japanese in any way, must be aware of the two realities simultaneously. I have been astonished at my colleagues' ignorance of Japan on many occasions, and particularly at the many Franco-Japanese or 'Western-Japanese' conferences I have attended. My astonishment has often greatly exceeded that of our Japanese partners, for it is a phenomenon to which experience has inured them. Far from separating economics from culture (as we all too often do), the Japanese have understood ever since the Meiji period (and even earlier) that to enter the world of Western science it is essential to understand and assimilate the West's culture. Japan has not changed her approach, and cultural information from the West is very quickly translated and made available to the general public, or at least to the specialists, no matter how little relevance it may appear to have.

Now the tables are turned, and it is the West which, like it or not, must come to terms with Japan. All things specifically Western, even things like fashions, wines and French Camembert, are being produced in Japan now and nobody can rest on his laurels. But this is not all. Now that the Japanese are selling the most typical Western products, they are actually creating the styles that are most typically Western, so that the centres of fashion, taste, and creativity are shifting from Paris, Milan, and New York over to Tokyo. In other words, they have looped the loop: they are selling the West to the West.

It is vital for us, then, to concern ourselves with the culture of Japan, whether traditional, classic, or modern, thereby responding to the Japanese as they themselves have always done to us.

In writing this book I have deliberately emphasized and perhaps even overemphasized certain concepts, expressing them in different ways in order to make their importance as clear as possible. For example: the notion of economic warfare, so very different from that of economic strategy. Whereas the mere adoption of a strategy still leaves open the possibility of mutual understanding in the pursuit of the general interest, in war, by contrast, everything is allowed in the struggle to defeat the enemy at any price. However, the meaning of behaviour is always related to a context, and that context may well be complex. The key to the Japanese context is the sense of national unity as symbolized by the person of the Emperor, the keystone of the whole nation. This fundamental hierarchy is the backbone, and it is important to understand how everything centres on it. The other key element in Japan is her tradition. Tradition means very ancient customs that command lasting respect and form the bedrock of society. But these customs, with their background in Shintoism, Buddhism, and Confucianism, are not everything. There exists in Japan an even deeper stratum, a stratum of ancient customs whose essence is purely shamanic. What has to be grasped is the undeniable fact that such 'customs' are still in evidence 2,000 years later in modern times. Indeed, the permanent mobilization of a 'pure and hard' Japan as a fervent and disciplined army would be inconceivable without some kind of safety-valve, a very deep dionysiac outlet allowing the Japanese to get rid of their tensions after a day's work at the office or in the factory; and Japanese life is astonishingly well organized for relaxation and the celebration of the senses. But how do the supremely contradictory powers in the Japanese soul actually manage to work together harmiously so as to energize a movement of such ceaseless creativity? It is as though the Japanese possess a peculiar genius of their own that somehow taps the very life-process itself and the sap of living things. Japan has a mysterious ability always to fall on her feet, like a cat, however catastrophic her situation: this ability is in fact linked both to her shamanic foundation and to Shinto tradition, which actually has no other programme than to venerate life and all its manifestations. This embraces birth, life, and death. The dynamic and creative centre is symbolized by the Confucian spirit, which involves a sense of duty, honour, and obligation (*giri*).

Fundamentally, the fact that each one participates in a collective entity implies that each one must do what he does as perfectly as possible. In this sense, living is justifiable. Equally, insofar as, for some deep reason, the necessity for living vanishes, dying is justifiable. This is what makes it so difficult to explain to a Western mind the generosity, the subtlety, and the implacability of the Japanese soul: and it is likewise extraordinarily difficult to show how shamanic, Shintoist, Buddhist, and Confucianist influences ultimately coalesce in a single whole.

A paradoxical situation inevitably engenders a book that itself seems no less paradoxical. But what we are actually grappling with are the visible and invisible sides of one and the same spirit; we are showing at once how the bow is stretched and how the arrow is shot, and the truth here is less paradoxical than it seems. For the very thing which is the key to Japanese strategy and Japanese success is actually a whole which cannot be dissected without our succumbing to the deceptive charms of over-simplification. There would be no point in composing a panegyric to Japan, any more than there would be in painting too negative a picture. Accepting reality as it is seems to be well-nigh impossible though, and the truth is that the best book will always ultimately remain a pale introduction by comparison with actual experience. All the same, I hope that these reflections, with their different levels and emphases, will be useful for all those who one day, for whatever reason, want to get to grips with the things which make Japan look just like another planet.

2. Yukio Mishima: Only what you cannot see is Japanese

It was the end of a sunny afternoon in December 1968. Accompanied by a French TV crew, I had just completed a long interview with Mishima Yukio. He was posing for a final photo-session on a terrace, looking out over endless rows of roofs. I was watching the perfectly defined lines of his face, as clear cut and sure as he himself seemed to be in each of his gestures and observations. I had in front of me a man who was calm, sober, and even grave. So what had happened to the extravagant image of the eccentric homosexual, the poseur who had had himself photographed as a naked Saint Sebastian riddled with arrows? And what about the smartly-dressed 'soldier', the leader of a private militia who was all the rage in the media? He was quite simply a highly-talented writer with a worldwide reputation who had recently discreetly refused the Nobel Prize for Literature so it could be given to his old friend and fellow-citizen Kawabata Yasunari. Courteously, he introduced me to his wife, a sweet, elegant little lady, and his two daughters. Then he invited me round to his home.

His house was about an hour from the centre of Tokyo and seemed curiously out of place in the middle of such perfectly banal suburbia. In the garden beside it, at the centre of a marble zodiac, he had placed a statue of Orpheus with a lyre in his left hand. The house itself, with its tall French windows, white balustrades, amphorae, dwarf palms, and terraces, looked like a comfortable and spacious villa on the Cote d'Azur. The ground floor, and this was the height of refinement and luxury for Japan, was furnished in the eighteenth century French style, while the large and spacious first floor, by contrast, had an ultra-modern décor.

I was somewhat surprised to discover such a décor in the home of a person widely known to symbolize, even in his very contradictions, the virtues of the Japanese soul. I asked him 'How do you explain the fact that the whole of your house contains nothing specifically Japanese?' Mishima Yukio smiled, and said, 'Here, only what you cannot see is Japanese.'

Nothing I have ever heard describes so perfectly the very soul of Japan. 'Only what you cannot see is Japanese.' Anyone who has the least acquaintance with this totally unique country will find that such a thought is naggingly and persistently present like a ceaseless vibration in its history, strategy, economics, poetry, religion, art, and politics. There is a hidden principle here, and it is this: the real force and the hidden source of the inner energy that crosses all bridges and breaks through all barriers is that which is neither said nor expressed nor written. No doubt this is also why lovers in Japan never utter the notoriously banal Western expression 'I love you'. Of course the word 'to love' is in the dictionary. It is *aishitemasu*. But saying it is incongruous or worse: indeed, it is almost a kind of shameless and obscene action. If two people are in love, they do not need words to say so: the tension in their being and their look, the touching of hands and the thousand sweet nothings of love are all the language that is needed, and it is a language that is at once universal, personal, and eloquent.

We know the poverty of words when it comes to expressing the nature of reality. The Japanese frequently use word-concepts. The definitions of these indicate a complex reality, a 'state of things', a 'state of being', or even a 'state of underlying reality'. Like these word-concepts, the meaning of Japanese efficiency both confronts and eludes the student of Japan. Westerners look with astonishment at this country which seems almost a brother, and yet the very closeness of the resemblance makes this brother both transparent and inaccessible. Perhaps no other country embodies quite so powerfully the ultra-sophisticated image of all-conquering science and technology. Even the USA is often beaten at its own game by Japan. When we think of the future, it is the word 'Nippon' that comes to mind. And yet, for all the fantastic revolutions that are taking place under the impact of this omnipresent invasion of hypertechnology, the traditional immutable depths of Japan have not changed and never will. There is in fact an implicit, hidden watchword in Japan: to be, to remain unchangeably Japanese in the face of all.

Indeed, by contrast with the dehumanized West, Japan possesses a national treasure, a soul that is an entity born from the primeval gods or *kami*. If not immortal, this soul is resolved to be invincible. Under the pressure of events, Japan may bow for a time, but up to now her history shows how she has remained, and probably will remain, unconquered. After Hiroshima and Nagasaki, the defeat of 1945 proves nothing.

After that first filmed interview, I went back to see Mishima. He gave me a whole evening for a man-to-man discussion, on condition that there was no camera, no tape recorder and no notebook. We were there to talk, with my interpreter as the sole witness.

For Mishima, the darkest day in Japan's history was the day when Emperor Hirohito addressed the nation in language that was both archaic and incomprehensible to almost every Japanese. A few minutes later the Emperor's address was translated clearly from the old language of the court, and millions of Japanese felt like committing harakiri. In fact hundreds of them did gather in front of the moats of the imperial palace and do precisely that. Before the speech was broadcast on the radio, a revolt broke out among army officers. All the traditional authority and *sang-froid* of the Japanese old guard, indeed of anyone in a leadership position, was needed to stop the country collapsing into chaos. For the first time in the whole history of the country, the Emperor had just spelt out that Japan was showing the white flag. The atomic bombs of Hiroshima and Nagasaki had got the better of her. It was a case of unconditional surrender to the USA. And the god-man, the most sacred man in the country, the Emperor, who was never heard and never seen, had just said so himself.

'At the age of 20', Mishima told me, 'I was a student and I worked in a Japanese naval yard. I felt saved when the war finished. But I was profoundly disturbed by the emperor's declaration that he was no longer a god. That seemed to me like a kind of treason, treason towards those who had died for him.'

What happened that day induced in Mishima the feeling that Japan had failed. She was no longer the Great Nippon, dear to all Japanese ultra-nationalists. He himself continued to dream of a Japan that was hard and pure. This is an extreme attitude but it is worth mentioning if only because it illustrates, in the perspective of Mishima's spectacular death, the extent to which nothing belongs solely to the past where this country is concerned, since all historical facts retain their impact and their meaning in a perpetual present.

Mishima was a descendant of a Samurai family, and in spite of his dali-esque eccentricities, he knew that he too must also respect a hidden code, a code of honour, which implies that no-one may criticize a superior unless he justifies it at the expense of his own life. He had waited a long time, pondering the memory of that unforgettable wound. All the more so, in that when he completed his studies and carried off the first prize at the famous University of Tokyo, the emperor himself had personally offered him a gold watch. To Mishima this seemed to constitute a personal bond with the Emperor, it strengthened his natural feeling of respect. And yet this did not eradicate the resentment he had gone on feeling deep down since the day of surrender. The result is well known: on 25 November 1970, Mishima Yukio invaded the staff headquarters of the Japanese army at the head of his private militia; one of his men killed a guard, while Mishima himself rushed into the chief of staff's office and held him at bay.

Leaning out of the window, he harangued the officers and troopers who had rushed up to see whether this eccentric writer, made famous by newspapers and television, was going to stage another publicity coup. But this time Mishima was in earnest, in fact tragically so. A few minutes later, observing the rules precisely, he carried out a perfect

1. Yukio Mishima in front of his private militia. The uniforms were designed by him.

seppuku, a ritual suicide which consists in plunging a short sword into the belly just below the navel, cutting upwards near the liver, and finally, without pulling the blade out, cutting downwards again to slice across the belly horizontally. His closest friend, who was at his side, beheaded him as prescribed by the ritual.

Three days before his *seppuku*, Mishima had delivered to his publisher the fourth volume of his last serialized novel. On the final page of the book he had written down the day of his death: 25 November 1970.

.2.   Mishima at home in 1968 during the interview.

It is as if Mishima were a kind of symbol of something invincible in the Japanese soul. In retrospect, his meticulously organized suicide, spectacular though it was, amounted to a perfectly traditional kind of protest. Beneath the calm violence of the act, we can discern the persistence of an invincible idea.

Of course, Mishima is far from being typical of the Japanese, but he does symbolize a profound truth about Japan, the Japan that is at once visible and invisible, the unconquerable Japan of which we shall be talking.

'For us', said a Japanese industrialist, '*budō*, the nō theatre, and *kabuki*, are nourishment, and the depths of our soul are very ancient.

So we can be modern or even ultra-modern without losing our roots. Nothing in Japan is isolated: the light taste of *sake* (rice wine), the savour of *sashimi* (raw fish), the respect in which we hold our traditions, and the veneration we offer our emperor, all this is one. The difference between us and the West is that we still have a centre, or what you call a soul. The centre is also the kernel. Without it, the fruit decays and dies.'

PART 1

1

THE STRATEGY
OF THE LABYRINTH

1. The taste of sake

Sake or rice wine is, as everyone knows, the national drink of the Japanese. During a meal it is considered good taste to pour a little wine for one's neighbours, since custom dictates that one does not serve oneself. Sake is also served in Shinto sanctuaries. It is a mark of homage to the gods or *kami* to appreciate the taste of sake. Enjoyment is derived not only from the drink itself but also from the highly variegated little earthenware cups in which it is served. The numerous ways in which saki is consumed symbolize the different moments of space-time continuum that is, like all things, at once both real and impermanent. The taste of each cup is indefinably unique and experienced differently; the taste of sake may recall cherry blossom or the contemplation of Mount Fuji. A deep sense of reality is accompanied by a perception of the content and the presence of reality the very moment each instant is experienced. Continuity, presence, and impermanence are three words which represent simultaneously a state of being, a state of the soul, and a way of mediation akin to the highly poetic expression of a *haiku*.[1]

That, too, is the essence of the strategy of the unseen. Every reality always has several levels instantaneously, and every state of being is by definition inexpressible. Because of this inward disposition the mind is both aerial and terrestrial. A man who cannot feel the subtle taste of each thing has, for the Japanese, a truly mediocre spirit. For lack of such a tradition, Westerners often fail to understand certain moments of silence, certain 'moments of abstraction' they encounter with the

---

[1] An epigrammatic Japanese verse form in seventeen syllables.

Japanese, who seem to be listening to them rather as if they were elsewhere, when in fact they are one hundred percent attentive to what is being said. One of our principal defects is always to want to 'understand' too quickly. To bring himself to the point of action, a Japanese needs a certain amount of time, he needs to distance himself, and then his decision will be dictated by considerations that seem to us to have minimal importance. His exquisite politeness can never say no. But his 'yes' may be capable of almost infinite interpretation. It may mean 'no' or 'perhaps' or 'wait we shall look into this', or perhaps an affirmatory yes which will mean 'I have understood you perfectly well, I am your friend, and I am in complete agreement with you!'

Many statistics are put out about the behaviour of the Japanese in all sorts of different areas, but it is vital not to draw over-hasty conclusions from them. Thus, for example, statistics about the importance of religion in the life of the Japanese are always very negative. The Japanese might look just like a population of atheists, whereas the truth is that they are in fact extremely religious. But when a Japanese answers precise questions, such as: 'Do you or do you not believe in the Buddha or in the *kami* or in Shinto?'—his replies do not really have any affirmative meaning. To expose oneself to being declared 'religious' is like showing a lack of modesty in relation to one's feelings when they are of a highly personal nature. Nothing is more difficult than to understand the feelings of people in a country where the collectivization of a whole society coexists with a very high degree of individualism. Words are only concepts, and concepts have innumerable facets and innumerable ways of being lived out. Birds experience the wind without knowing the wind, the fish swims in the water without knowing the water. Reality does not need to be defined; if it is defined, all we are left with is a definition which has been substituted for reality. Thus the apparent abstraction of a Japanese may in fact be an extraordinary attentiveness, while all our techniques for analysis and concentration may seem to a Japanese like a tremendous unreality.

The Japanese are hidden from our sight, they see without being seen. And what is it that hides them? A persistent and millenary tradition that we no longer have, a different mode of thought that is accessible to very few Westerners. It is the source of an art of strategy inspired by laws and principles alien to us, originating in the old samurai schools, principles from the Confucian and Shinto traditions and from Zen wisdom. A corpus of principles containing teaching about a way of feeling, thinking, and acting from a central point.

Japan, it has often been said, is waging an economic war on the West. A complex, low-key war, but implacable and pitiless. The extraordinary mobilization of the Japanese in the interests of this economic warfare has its reasons; and though they have their contemporary dimension, these reasons are chiefly historical. To understand Japan means to know how an adversary thinks and acts. Indeed, it means being transformed a little oneself, for understanding from the outside is useless. Because he fails to penetrate the deeper meaning of the Japanese tradition and the Japanese spirit, the westerner is in danger of being definitively relegated to the bottom of the class.

Thus everything is to be gained by arriving at an understanding of the riches of this tradition. There are several levels on which we may investigate 'the strategy of the unseen' and it has several meanings: from economic espionage to information super-networks, these mirror the very soul of the Japanese at its deepest and most admirable. Japan is certainly a cunning and pitiless adversary, but if the battle is to be on equal terms, we must above all assimilate her spirit and appreciate it.

Very few books build a bridge between the old Japan and the Japan of today. Such books need to be just a little like adventure stories and even in a sense like collections of poetry. There is so much to be learnt by the student, the businessman, the lover of unchanging traditions and the company boss. If we look not only at the economic aspects of the present day but also at the immensely poetic and mysterious sides of the Japanese soul, we find that Japanese realism and dynamism have their roots in concepts which may seem unreal and imponderable. But that is precisely the secret. The two sides must not be separated. As for history, it is there to show us the essentially unchanged nature of the Japanese soul and Japanese strategy.

A recent example has shown me the extent to which things outside time are always of present importance. In November 1984, I took part in an international colloquium, 'Ways of knowing', organized with the help of France-Culture at the University of Tsukuba. Confronted on this occasion with Western scientists steeped in a robust positivism and pragmatism, the Japanese persisted to a man in expounding the old concept of *ki*. What this amounts to is a traditional view of the world conceived as a perfect harmony. *Ki* also designates

3.   Takizo Higuchi, grand master of the Maniwa-nen school. At the moment of the attack he utters a cry, the *kiai*.

human and cosmic energy. They were expressing a philosophical and even a metaphysical view of things in response to the prudent and purely scientific approach of the Westerners. In fact the divide between the two approaches was considerable. The Westerners, baffled and curious, made a sincere effort to come to terms with Japanese thought. But the exchange was reduced to a monologue. The Japanese understood what the Western scientists were saying, but the understanding was not mutual. Neither concepts nor approach nor conclusions provided a basis for agreement. They tried to understand one another through analogies and comparisons.

But how could *ki* be adapted to the western scientific approach? How could two opposing cultures and philosophies be reconciled? Rationalist western culture finds its spiritual values in transcendence. The natural culture of the Japanese is marked by its shamanic origin and finds its values in immanence. It is creation which reflects the divine. A detailed analysis could easily show how Western culture has been cut off from its own tradition since the thirteenth century and has fallen into a rationalist pragmatism which has paradoxically turned into an idealist pragmatism. Japan, on the other hand, has never lost that sense of what is real, a feel for the living world as it actually is. With her unity goes a pragmatic realism that is 'naturally efficient', if I may put it like that. A way of conceiving the nature of reality is also a way of having or not having influence over reality. A Japanese philosopher friend put the question this way: 'Our culture is the result of an intimate knowledge of the laws of nature, at the point where rational and irrational aspects meet. Westerners have "points of view" about things. We Japanese have certain feelings about what things are. So while you go about analyzing and dividing up arguments, we are bringing them together. Our vantage-point is not the same. While Westerners are looking at a problem from where they stand, we shall be looking at it from several floors higher up; we shall be happily looking down at the vantage-point of the westerners below us.'

This is absolutely fundamental if we are to understand Japan. It must be appreciated that the pragmatic Japanese mind and its efficiency come out of the non-dualism inherent from the beginning in Japan's original religion, Shintoism. This is of paramount importance for, to a Japanese brought up in the traditional culture, dualism has no meaning. It is very difficult for him to understand what can be the significance of two things in isolation. And yet Shinto is far from being a monotheistic religion: it perceives the one through the multiple, and although it does acknowledge a creator, he only appears through myriad *kami* or spirits. Thus the Japanese can call himself secular in the sense that he knows how the divine is brought to man, rather than in the sense that he has spiritual aspirations. To be spiritual in Japan it is sufficient to be sensitive to the nature of things as they are in themselves, to understand their necessity, their form and their essence, in other words, what they are made for.

In tune with an eternal continuity, the Japanese also has a direct relationship with the eternal present. He is present wholly in what he is and in what he does. This is the meaning of the expression 'here and now' which is found both in Shinto and in Zen Buddhism. These concepts may seem abstract to Western minds in which all arguments arise from a process of rationalistic reasoning which overrides everything else. And if the face of the world was not changing it would no doubt be possible to be content with that way of thinking. But from now on we shall be increasingly obliged to reckon with the power and growing supremacy of an Asia whose rather different mentality is, as it were, short-circuiting our most well-tested methods.

As for Japan, she has every chance of becoming the first world power by the year 2000. If it is the case that abstract concepts have a concrete influence, if market techniques too depend on a way of thinking, there is nothing superfluous about learning to think a little differently. When in discussion the sharp definitions of rational minds come up against the blur, uncertainty and 'non-visible element' in the Japanese mind, it is quite pointless to bang at the doors and hit out in the fog. The Japanese market will remain a protected citadel in the face of all comers. Is this Machiavellianism? No. Yet how can we explain the way they take over markets all around the world while keeping their own closed? Their politicians and business men do their best to make the rest of the world suffer patiently, apparently only yielding when the pressure becomes too strong.

Of course a Japanese market does exist. But it has a different quality from that of western markets. A really determined effort to break into it would presuppose changes in the whole structure of Japanese society itself: for it is a society in which all the commercial structures are at the same time organic structures bound up with one another not simply by common interests but also by a whole texture of friendships, understandings, rights, obligations, and co-responsibility which are part of a typically Japanese background. Foreign companies will never establish their own distribution networks and undertake any sort of commercial expansion in Japan itself, without the prior agreement of the Japanese and without the business in question being under Japanese control. The truth is that Japan cannot be conquered either by weapons or by trade. And her structures are so homogeneous that no political power can alter that situation.

Thus there is no other solution but to grapple with the Japanese mentality and to understand the subtlety and patience required to collaborate with the Japanese in opening up their markets. But this requires a willingness to abandon at least a part of one's rationalistic mentality for the sake of gaining more information and a greater depth of culture, and of becoming both more sensitive and a better listener.

The West is currently in an extremely delicate situation: our situation resembles the illustration of the serpent biting its own tail. The crisis has its own inner momentum, and the Asians are happy to aggravate it. There is nothing easier for them than to follow martial arts practice, that teaches them to hold on to the enemy and lead him by his own rhythm.

While the West goes to sleep in the midst of its own crises and disputes, the Asiatics step up their rhythm and pour out at an ever-increasing rate the consumer products with which they inundate the West. The secret of this game is at one and the same time to hold the enemy off one's own markets, to conquer his, and to put oneself in a strong position to deal with a crisis. Options must be widened in the interests of better resistance: the ultimate goal must be kept in mind constantly: and just the right moment for scoring points must be waited for. That is what Japan in particular is doing, and it is also what will be done soon by other 'awakening' countries of Asia like China and Korea. The economic and commercial struggle is only the cloak that conceals a struggle of minds, cultures and concepts that are diametrically opposed.

As the Western nations sink deeper and deeper into a state of crisis, paralysing themselves in their growing balance of payment deficits, their social conflicts and inter-party battles, the Asiatic countries will speed up their advance. Beaten at her own game, in accordance with a strategy devised by non-dualist minds, the West will perhaps learn in her turn the delicate art of archery and even the art of shooting without looking at the target.

2. Tradition and the future

Let us imagine a businessman (if he can be called that) of the twelfth or thirteenth century in France—a builder of cathedrals say—and a Japanese businessman of today. They would have no difficulty in understanding each other. In ways that are barely any different, despite outward appearances, both share in the same tradition. The medieval man was perhaps a Templar. Before he could undertake a project as vast as the Cathedral at Chartres, for example, he had to be by turns a financier, a haulage contractor, an architect, and a leader of men. He had to get the craft guilds together and devise some cunning means of persuading them all to operate harmoniously together in the smooth running of the project.

Technical and scientific qualities went together in the framework of a traditional culture, a culture conceptually very distant from our own, modern-day society. The cathedrals, as people are always quick to point out, are masterpieces of faith. True, yet this was not an idealized faith but a highly pragmatic one, a faith which integrated man into one single totality, envisaging him as an image of a whole that reflected in all its parts the stable laws of the universe: microcosm and macrocosm. Faith arises from a feeling that the divine and all that comes from the divine are in harmony. Harmony is itself the result of a coherent alchemy that unites contradictory forces so as to reveal them in all their creative stability. Architecture integrates stability and movement, it reflects the high and the low, and this harmony is both visible and invisible. It is an implicit prayer, the prayer of stones, numbers and proportions. In actual fact, here we have the very philosophy of *ki* and of harmony that the Japanese scientists were talking about at Tsukuba.

In sixteenth- and seventeenth-century Europe rationalists did their work, dualism became established and soon the 'scientific' spirit developed. The laws of nature were no longer understood except in their causes and effects. The world of forms, rhythms and proportions in relationship with man vanished. Nature was now nothing more than a décor. Rousseau and Voltaire became the gurus of the French. The West was lost without even knowing it. Only now is that beginning to be understood.

Every traditional civilization, on the other hand, including the Japanese, is based on the same concept of harmony. Every part, however tiny, is always a reflection of the whole, while there is a vision of the centre as source of creative dynamism. This is an integrating force which unifies all other energies and make them converge. There is no separation, no classification, nor even any analytically objective system in which the part is separated from the whole. Physical and material values interpenetrate with psychic and spiritual ones. A society of this kind, whether industrial or political, is organized in such a way that each one is in his place. In fact, centre and hierarchy create a structure as dynamic as life itself. All the molecules are organized from a central nucleus. And this is a valid model for tradition. As a traditional society, Japan still has a fairly close resemblance to this model. The Japanese are mysterious insofar as they possess the kind of global and integrated vision of all things that we no longer have. But such modes of being and thinking cannot be explained; they are like discussions concerning the limits of science and metaphysical concepts. That which *is* participates simply in the stable laws of the living world and in the nature of the real. But how can we bring the innumerable implications of these principles from the East to the attention of the West?

The Japanese may be perfectly at home here with something that is a familiar part of themselves, but such is unhappily not the case for us, even if it was once. It may well be true that the new physics has unwittingly come round to agreeing with traditional sources and is rediscovering in its procedures the concept of the unity of energies and the vision of a coherent universe, but we are, to be truthful, a long way from comprehending it . The new physics is still the domain of a few initiates. A rediscovery of the fundamental importance of the Creator is perhaps necessary to change the nature of our society and give it a new stability: a global rather than a partial vision of man and the cosmos, of the living world and its laws, of nature and the respect due to it.

How do the Japanese themselves apply this philosophy of harmony? Let us take as an example the doyen of Japanese industry chiefs. His name is Matsushita Kōnosuke. At the time of writing, in 1985, he is 90 years old. His industrial empire predates even Idemitsu (Sony)—it was the earliest in modern Japan (1918)—assuming we leave out of consideration the great *zaibatsu* such as Mitsubishi, established about 100 years ago, or Mitsui, founded in the sixteenth century. Matsushita has set up a college, the Matsushita College of Government and Management, whose aim is both to teach and to research 'a new philosophy of government and management based on a new conception of man'. He publishes a monthly journal, *PHP* (Peace, Happiness, Prosperity), intended to establish 'a forum for a better world'. In reality, 'new' here means 'traditional'. Or rather, a new understanding of our world in the light of traditional teachings. In this enterprise we see the ancient immutable Japan reappearing in modern clothing, adapted for the modern mind, and especially for the Japanese.

Marketing strategy is in some ways analogous with the laws of war. And here, too, the Japanese are way ahead. Nothing is easier for the Japanese than to 'reflect' the western mentality, which is ultimately very easy to analyze. The Japanese are unbeatable at this game of mirrors. By contrast, the inability of westerners to penetrate the Japanese mentality drives them to all sorts of different reactions, ranging from curiosity to exasperation. This is sometimes expressed in outbursts such as 'Either they collaborate or it's war!', or 'Either they open up their markets or we close ours!'. Such reactions are simplistic and the Japanese analyzed and evaluated them a long time ago. Their

4.   Kōnosuke Matsushita at the age of 88. An industrial empire built on
     a dual foundation. A philosophy of business allied to the wisdom of life.

reply is 'Do as we do!' What this really means is 'Understand our
methods and adopt them!' It is easy to say, but how? We may analyze
Japanese companies and their management as much as we like, they
still hold the whip hand, freely establishing their businesses in

our own countries, and succeeding even on terrain which has been a graveyard for their rivals. This proves at least that their methods are exportable, so why are we so unable to adopt them?

The truth is that we are hampered by a widely accepted but misleading concept: that of industrial civilization. In fact, these two terms are mutually contradictory. There is no civilization except where there exists a highly elaborated culture which integrates all aspects of life, including art, poetry, and of course a philosophy of the laws of living beings. The Japanese as a people possess a mentality that assumes a cluster of values which we do not, or do not any longer, have in the West. There is nothing to be gained by giving in to instinctively defensive or racist reactions. We are not dealing with anything esoteric or magic. Our own culture possesses infinite riches: it is perfectly feasible for us to align ourselves with Japanese culture while maintaining our own specificity. If we can rediscover the sources of our own culture, a culture forgotten for seven centuries, we shall find we have a language in common with the Japanese. The example of the twelfth-century cathedral builder who would be perfectly comprehensible to a twentieth-century Japanese manager is not a paradox. But we for our part no more understand what made the cathedral builder tick seven centuries ago than we understand the Japanese manager who appears to think and act as we do now. The extent of our Western defeat is striking when we look at it through Asiatic eyes. Analyses like 'They are more productive because they work like beavers' are not very helpful if we are going to make any progress.

Whether we like it or not, we must abandon our quantitative ways of thought and get back to qualitative thinking, then everything else— (i.e. success) will follow. But the dialogue of the deaf is likely to continue until the West finally admits defeat, until we are thoroughly beaten and are at last ready to concede that there is another 'solution'. There is a third way between Capitalism and Marxism. It is a way of return to the sources which eliminates all types of dualism and simplistic rationalism. The nature of living things is both extraordinary in its complexity and admirable in its simplicity. No society can last unless it reflects the properties of living beings and unless it rediscovers the laws that govern them, in order to apply these in the interests of the general prosperity as well as of the particular happiness of each individual.

This may appear Utopian to those who have not understood that society must be organized not on the basis of a succession of revolutions, but on stable principles which accept, as nature herself does, all those possibilities for change and all those apparent revolutions which are actually nothing but the mark of a constant adaptation to 'that which is becoming'. It is the eternal image of the tree of life or the spiral or the relationship between point and circle. These are not simply empty symbols, they are models that illustrate the fundamental energy of all things.

The Japanese can sing a hymn to their firm every morning. This makes each one a responsible part of the whole. Global vision is the irresistible dynamic present in everything. It allows for growth and becoming, it puts each individual thing and each gesture in its place. A 'human machine' cannot be integrated into a firm. What is to be integrated in this way is a whole, a creature with mind, feelings, and flesh.

Having said all this, access to the right ideas does not necessarily guarantee right thinking. Our civilization is what it is. In the history of civilizations it may even come to be seen as a cancerous growth on the human spirit. There is nothing novel about saying that we are playing at being sorcerer's apprentices, and that our model of civilization is probably a monstrous absurdity. Everything we undertake is definitively based on quantity. The extraordinary dynamics of modern societies is like a steamroller destabilizing and crushing everything in its way. The enormous quantities of money invested by the 'advanced' countries conceal highly fragile structures. But this very fragility is a weapon for the colonization of 'developing' countries. Contemporary economics, based on development and expansion at any price, exploits whatever is to hand. The fascinating possibilities for progress that are opening up in biotechnology, in computer science, and in the use of nuclear power, are two-headed monsters, and there is always the possibility that one of the heads might devour us. But this book does not claim to be anything more than an analysis of various levels of a society which manifests an exemplary corporate intelligence and productiveness. If we desire to look at things as they are, and our society today as it is within the framework of reality, Japan offers us the vision of an uncommon balance between tradition and modernity.

The mere fact that we have so much to learn and so much to understand does not of course mean that Japan is the paradigm of all the virtues. Like all that is human, Japan has her scandals, her pressure groups, her monstrous hobbies. There is even a 'Japan of cruelty', as I have sometimes called it, of which numerous examples could be given. To name but one, there is the case of the pitiless harshness of Japanese institutions during the War. In fact, Nipponese nationalism, whether military or economic, has extremist sides which need to be understood. When the different clans used to make war on each other, they would slaughter each other without mercy. And today Japan is still the expression of an ambivalence between the harshness of the feudal spirit, which lingers on even now, and the deeper nature of the Japanese people, which is extremely sensitive and sentimental. Hence the existence of an exaggerated individualism in conjunction with a group mentality. In other words, a combination of very ancient conservative characteristics with a modern progressive spirit.

We are accustomed to regard the samurai as invincible warriors. And so they were, as long as it was part of their 'vocation', which was primarily to be fighters. But the true samurai ideal was that of the fully-rounded personality—far from being primitive brutes, these were often extremely refined and highly educated men. That did not prevent them from combining exquisite sensitivity with pitiless behaviour in war or in inter-clan struggles. But it is precisely this paradox of extreme gentleness combined with extreme harshness that explains the fascination of the Japanese soul, with all its prodigious contrasts.

Impassibility in the face of death becomes ferocity in warfare. In the theatre, the cinema, and in real life this results in instances of intensely dramatic behaviour that is by turns exquisite and tragic, horrible and admirable. This vast distance between the extremes is what constitutes the substance of the Japanese soul, its invisible element. In the name of reason it is possible to go beyond all reason. Equally, every passion can be brought under the law of reason.

Duty and rhythm, the spirit of duty and a mysterious feel for life perpetually interact within the Japanese soul as two forces that are contradictory but related. In every sphere the imponderable element derives from the resolution of extremes, so that what we see is actually a concerted spontaneity, as if the extremes of freedom were born out of the extremes of rigour.

Perhaps all this still seems abstract. But what we are saying about

5. A kabuki actor: kabuki is theatre of great power and magnificence.

the inmost depths of the Japanese soul is as applicable today to the
practice of the martial arts as it is to business. All the martial arts
are based on a sense of rhythm and space-time, on mastery of the
centre, on a quasi-alchemical feeling for the complex energies of nature
and consequently on an apprenticeship in their integration. When
respiration becomes 'breath', when movement becomes the manifestation of harmony, when one learns to be neither slow nor quick, when
concentration gives way to a kind of sixth sense, then one begins to
understand what the martial arts are really about.

In the West, our thought structure is essentially dualist. We are
always contrasting this with that, we separate ideas in arguments,
we are forever isolating the part from the whole. As a rule, the
Japanese—and Easterners in general—do precisely the opposite. Our
logic finds this mentality illogical or incomprehensible, because we
have separated the mind from the body, the body from nature, and
nature from life. The more we rely on ready-made concepts and ideas
to make progress, the deeper we wallow in our own demagogy. This
demagogy we substitute for a doctrine or a philosophy, until it collapses
on us. Then we say that the model we selected was the wrong one,
and we pick out another one, only it turns out to have the same defects
under different labels. In other words, reason, planning and research,

(whether sociological, political, or economic), have no power if they do not concentrate on any one point, or if the focal point aimed at by market constraints, pressure groups, parties and insititutions, is arbitrary rather than strategic.

In the face of our frequently absurd divisions, the notorious Japanese consensus makes possible a strategy of delicate subtlety. The Western complex about the Japanese is the result of an isolation created by a culture that is not a culture. The Japanese consensus rests first and foremost on a homogeneous culture that is still bound up in great measure with recognizable and unvarying properties, and this could be rather clumsily expressed by saying that they have a deep understanding of the true nature of reality: and they are supremely certain that reality is not dualist. The confrontation between East and West is that of a dualist and a non-dualist way of thinking. We have not really managed to come to grips with all the consequences of this, indeed we do not really possess the means to analyze it.

In the medium term, an incoherent ideology is bound to be mastered by a coherent one. Our task, which is difficult, is to take this confrontation of two mentalities and demonstrate the balance of forces, or at least to indicate the strengths on the Japanese side. Will we gain anything from this exercise? Will it enable us to improve our own performance? Are such contrasts of light and shade really instructive? A non-dualist type of thought can very easily understand a dualist way of thinking and successfully manipulate it by exploiting all its defects. That is what the Japanese do, and they do it with consummate skill. If we analyze the question closely, we can see that for us, Japan is an almost impenetrable monolithic entity. And yet all the time, under the protection of their language, their habitual secrecy, the thousand forms of their culture, the Japanese are ceaselessly subjecting the West to meticulous surveys. Our information about Japanese companies is qualitatively hugely inferior to what the Japanese know about our companies: while the West is subjected to constant and relentless observation, Japan continues to be like a virtually impenetrable shell.

Getting to grips with Japan, therefore, does not simply mean finding out the similarities between ourselves and Japan, but understanding the differences. Of course the Japanese themselves are not at all keen to supply us with the key to these differences. They believe we are incapable of understanding them. They make not the slightest effort to explain, and this is because deep down they are highly sensitive about that which in their culture is typically Japanese. They find themselves in a situation which in many respects eludes all analysis. For they are not mentally accustomed to consider their own customs and the traditional aspects of their culture from an analytical and critical point of view. Finally, moreover, there is in them a strain of racism which impels them deliberately to draw a veil over their own impenetrable Japan, a country where the foreigner is still only tolerated with considerable reservations.

Such paradoxical remarks on the Japanese mentality could be multiplied *ad infinitum*: it is so easy to give contradictory descriptions of them all in the same breath. But the two analyses will in fact complement one another and will bring to light a new reality. Thus the Japanese are at one and the same time pragmatic and irrational, non-mystical and yet heavily committed to the religious; they are pagan and profane while preserving a feeling for the sacred, they are efficient even while addicted to ancient superstitions. Their individualism is an emanation of their group spirit, their harshness is equalled only by an almost excessive emotivity and sensitivity, the expression of a double entity that is both feminine and masculine. The solitary soul of the samurai is a good reflection of this. There a sense of the fragility of everything; the impermanence and the transitoriness symbolized by the cult of cherry-blossom is combined with a certain insensitivity and indeed a cruel harshness, as we have said, when duty and obedience demand it.

There are many reasons why the Japanese only feel comfortable when they are among themselves, why they are so reticent about accepting foreigners, including other Asians, why even among themselves misunderstandings often arise, why they manifest so many different types of behaviour within the small compass of their country, why they have so many different festivals and local traditions, and how so many diversities ultimately blend into a common background. The Japanese accept all the economic, cultural, sociological, and religious points of view that are attributed to them without ever recognizing themselves more than partially in each of these. The co-existence within them of the worst and the best, the most atrocious bad taste with the most exquisite beauty, an immense tolerance and an almost unique capacity for understanding, together with a deeply-rooted insularity and chauvinism, along with so many other equally sharply contrasting traits, means that the Japanese only really feel happy among themselves; consequently they never think it useful to analyze their own image. Imagine an ocean that is simultaneously raging and calm, or a monster swallowing-up passers-by while children play happily next to it. Such images short-circuit common sense. It is hard to imagine Westerners living without common sense, but in Japan there is simply the natural feeling for things, combining, as we have said, the rational and the irrational.

More extensive analysis would show us that what we call common sense the Japanese would call 'a feeling for what is' or 'balance'. That what we call 'analysis' would be 'vision' in their terms. That the word 'efficiency' ought to be translated by 'dedication' and 'communion'. And that terms as obvious as 'good' and 'evil' would be translated as 'purity' and 'impurity' or 'harmony' and 'disharmony'. If we stay within our world-view we have no bait attractive enough to lure the Japanese fish. It glides eternally through waters which seem barred to us. They form an invisible, insurmountable barrier of contradiction, and no Western analysis is going to cross that barrier in a hurry.

Should we shrug our shoulders and say: 'Let's stop trying to understand, since we are perfectly certain we shall not succeed?' It is true that we do have an unavoidable handicap, namely, that we are not Japanese. Indeed, I would say that no-one can ever become Japanese. This is true, even if fate has decreed that you should be fascinated by Japan, 'Japanicized' to excess, even if you were to spend your life wanting to live in Japan and become integrated into Japanese life. There is a famous example, that of Lafcadio Hearn the writer, who was a naturalized Japanese with a Japanese wife and who wrote innumerable books on the most delicate and exotic aspects of Japanese life. He made himself Japanese, but lived out his last years in solitary sadness, rejected even by those to whom he had consecrated his life, his brilliant intelligence and his whole soul. We are forced to conclude that the fascination of Japan brings with it a virus that for some is incurable; they can no longer live anywhere but in Japan and in Japanese fashion. But that is unquestionably a disease, and one is never cured of wanting to become Japanese.

To tell the truth, the Japanese like differences. They appreciate it enormously when their hints and allusions are understood, when their admirable side is perceived and respected. At the same time, they want each to remain himself. A person is at liberty to adopt Japanese customs and styles as long as he preserves his own specificity, his own basic being, so to speak. Any kind of conversion, even at the highest level, becomes suspect. The best way to be marginalized or even rejected is to try too hard or want to do everything as they do. Provided this precondition is respected, however, there is a key available. It is the key of sensitivity, with all that word implies: a willingness to understand, an openness of mind, a restraint on the tendency to be critical, respect for customs. The best possible situation in Japan is that of the privileged guest, someone of whom people say that 'he honours Japan'. This is a wonderful gateway, for such a person finds there is no limit to the generosity and attentiveness of his Japanese friends. The less he expects, the more they will give him. His particular qualities and personality, together with a measure of warm-heartedness, delicacy, and humour, will win him solid and lasting friendships. He will certainly receive more than he can give. He must be like a supple dancer, relaxed and smiling on the razor's edge: firm when necessary and conciliatory when appropriate. The following actions are generally regarded as unforgivable; to make a friend or partner lose face; to be untrue to one's word and to break one's promises; to be lacking in respect and a sense of honour. In a word, to be lacking in what is commonly called the heart's wisdom.

In such a book as this, it would be pretentious to claim to be able to supply all the keys to the hidden Japan, just as it would be pointless to try and describe in words the sensation provoked by a phenomenon that invades every zone of one's sensibility. Each observation is itself like one facet of a reality which will be reflected in its turn in different forms. Nothing can replace direct experience, however limited it may be. Hopefully, these reflections will in their turn become the opportunity for the reader to discover for himself the riches of this country.

I shall conclude this section by drawing attention to some facts that may seem rather obvious. Putting a stethoscope to a patient's chest, drawing a bow, preparing tea or planning the launch of a new product are all actions that necessitate a knowledge of the body, of its organs and of the practical or underlying relationships between them. The art of archery requires mastery of the bow, of the correct stance, of the position of the arrow, and of the lining up of the target. The launch of a product requires information about market potential, the novelty of the product, the nature of probable rival products, production costs, marketing, etc. But what really matters is a person's attitude of mind when faced with a problem. Strategy is without strategy and tactics are without tactics. It might make more sense if we said 'Do what you have to do when you do it.' The Japanese way of reasoning may sometimes seem absurd to us, but it does in fact embody an obvious fact. What it really means is that one is *in* what one does. In any question or in any state of affairs, what must be eliminated are the paralyzing contradictions. The ultimate goal is always an ensemble of complex inner attitudes, whose consequence is to make us act with the greatest possible spontaneity and efficiency. This is the opposite of the Western didactic procedure. Every action is assimilated either slowly or quickly, but always as if innumerable models could be resolved into one single fundamental one. When the time comes to take a decision, it has to be taken, whatever the cost. The decision is an all-embracing commitment. No decision can go against the general consensus. However, within the framework of this consensus, each one is free to define his own style. Thus the style will define the man and in certain cases will establish someone as a *sensei*, a master who is universally respected.

Such is the functioning of their subtle energy, depending on a consensus of reciprocal rights and duties. Within Japanese society there exists a tremendous trust at all levels, from the humblest to the grandest. Each one puts his heart into doing what he does as conscientiously as possible.

The well-known high quality of Japanese products comes from the amazing security that derives from this mutual trust. It is clearly the result of a long tradition. But above all it stems from something quite clearly unique, the fact that the Japanese are a people nourished by the feeling that they belong to a privileged race, as if each Japanese belonged to one and the same single great family.

3. Information strategy

It is difficult to produce statistics in such a domain, but Japan is certainly one of the two or three best informed countries in the world. In all areas, but especially in the economic and scientific sectors, there is a veritable cult of information.

The Japanese boss is probably the best informed businessman in the world. For a long time now the Japanese have been basing their

6. The Tsukuba Exhibition. The telephone of the future. The image of
   the other person is an aid to mutual understanding . . . provided we
   look at it.

strategy on the most sophisticated analyses of their rivals. Whether their
methods are obvious, suspected, or secret, they are always powerful.
They consider all means of gaining information legitimate. A whole
network of their telex bases criss-cross the entire planet. These telexes
are all linked to computers situated in different centres, especially those
of the *shosha* or holding companies, and these computers receive the
information and analyse it. The chief such centre is the all-powerful
MITI, the Ministry for Commerce and Industry, which coordinates
the mass of information and transmits it to even the smallest Japanese
firms. Established on 25 May, 1949, *MITI* today employs 14,000

persons. Its offices are located at Kasumigaseki, in the heart of Tokyo's administrative district, and they sprawl over the whole of the archipelago. Other organizations, such as *JETRO*, which is involved with foreign trade, and *JICA*, an agency for international cooperation, together with about twenty other establishments, contribute to this flow of information. Furthermore, all embassies abroad act sectorally as channels (from America, Oceania, Eastern Europe and the USSR, China and South-East Asia) of information about everything that is happening abroad. Business, technology, advertising, politics, nothing escapes the analysis of the thousands of Japanese civil servants.

Just as the CIA watches over the military security of the USA, so *MITI* watches over Japan's economic security. This allows for a strategy of extraordinary suppleness and effectiveness. From day-to-day and hour-to-hour, everything is known about monetary fluctuations, movements on foreign markets, and new initiatives launched by rivals. *MITI* both coordinates all the information that might be of interest to industrialists, suggests appropriate political or strategic orientations and also watches over the application of strategy.

Cooperating closely with the powerful federation of the *Keidandren*, which is an association of industry chiefs, and with the Minister of Finance, *MITI* directs initiatives, blocks or releases credits, reinforces weak points, organizes united projects and either funds them or denies them credit.

Equally, all the big companies possess their own information networks. Ten percent of the working expenses of Mitsui-Bussan or Mitsubishi-Shoji, which are *shosha*, goes on communications. Mitsubishi has 125 telex bases across the world and 60 in Japan, all linked up to a computer. Its communications network covers 450,000 kilometres, a distance 11 times as great as the diameter of the earth. In France alone, where there are about 30,000 Japanese living (as compared with 2,400 French people in Japan), at least 1,000 of them devote themselves exclusively to gathering information.

Other researchers analyze all the specialized publications and official reports appearing in different parts of the world. Where necessary, they will go on field trips in order to complete a particular study, or else obtain theses done by researchers and academics. Without analysis, information is useless. The great majority of executives are specially trained. The high-flyers are sent abroad to learn languages and soak themselves in the customs and mentalities of different countries. On the other hand, every Japanese is suspicious of foreigners who can read and understand Japanese. A well-conceived strategy consists in knowing everything about one's rival while shrouding oneself in secrecy.

It is fair to say that the Japanese are doing well in all sectors. Each sector is constantly subjected to minute investigation. Japanese companies are never content with one study, they have half a dozen done by different firms and different people, each with a different brief, so as to obtain the maximum amount of information.

To have information on the adversary, to understand his mind, to foresee his reactions, is to have real power over him. At the same time, information is a cheap and straightforward source of wealth. As it happens, the West is generous with information at all levels. The Japanese are colonizing the West by the gradual conquest of the areas they know best. So relentless is this process that the Japanese will eventually be exporting western fashions to Westerners themselves. They are forever making minute examinations of the different sectors. It would be impossible to describe this phenomenon exhaustively. The truth is that there is no domain, from the smallest to the grandest, from the publishing of postcards or books to the fields of law, philosophy and literature, in which the Japanese are not either actually beating or preparing to beat the West, using the enormous mass of raw materials or finished products they have been gathering as a launching pad. Thus all the major French law theses, often hard to find even in France itself, because they are published by different universities, are to be found translated and collected in the Supreme Court in Tokyo. The same is true for Italian, American, and other such theses, and it is equally valid for scientific, economic, and sociological theses.

Likewise, the Japanese are the biggest buyers of licences in the world, yet they themselves are mightily reluctant to part with any of their own licences and patents. At any specialist exhibition, whether of fashion, cars, techology, manufactured goods or whatever, the Japanese are always present in numbers, and armed with all the necessary information to boot.

Who are these omnipresent Japanese? Very often they are students, but also executives, young graduates from Japanese universities or else executives promoted directly from within Japanese firms. After a few years in a company, the brightest of them are sent on expenses-paid visits abroad. They go to France, Germany, Italy, and especially to the US, where they enrol in universities, follow courses in business, or become integrated in all kinds of ways into the economic and cultural texture of the country. They make relationships, learn the language of the country, and study the mentality of its people.

On the occasion of a seminar organized by the review *l'Expansion* on the theme 'Understanding Japan', M. Pierre Baudry, Manager of a communications and marketing company in Japan, came and spoke about information techniques in Japan. Someone present at the seminar asked the inevitable question: 'Are all methods of obtaining information allowable?' M. Baudry answered, 'I think I can say that all methods are allowable.'

One example of this approach is that of the Japanese company Hitachi, convicted of industrial espionage against IBM by the American courts. A complex business, in which it seems that the CIA played a significant part, setting up a 'hit' operation to ensnare Hitachi. The Japanese company apparently had not only to pay a very substantial sum to IBM, but also to promise to report to IBM all future Japanese economic espionage to which they might be privy.

7.   Traditional snapshot of the school outing to the Buddhist Temple of Kiyomizu-dera at Kyoto.

'It's true the Japanese are dynamic' said M. Baudry, 'but after all, we have only to do the same as they do: answer them point by point and balance their efforts in everything. The Japanese know how to make the best of all that we have to offer and they exploit our "weaknesses".'

For instance, there are 300 scholarships on offer for Japanese students to go to France every year, but only 30 for French students to go to Japan.

Getting information and inspiration, assimilating a product or a culture—as far back as one can go in Japanese tradition this has been a constant feature. In the Tokugawa period, when Japan was closed to the West for two centuries, a limited amount of information continued to filter through from the West, even though Japan herself, with the exception of the Nagasaki enclave, remained hermetically sealed. The end result was a hypertrophy of the means of reception, together with a deliberate determination to block all opportunities for exchange. Japanese protectionism sometimes reaches almost incredible levels. Every Japanese who tries to import a product competing directly with what is home produced, unless the product somehow clearly serves the nation's interest, is quickly called to order by the civil servants at *MITI*. Emigration to Japan is achieved only with great difficulty. Protectionism extends to each single would-be immigrant, for each is interrogated exhaustively. Only those few whose fame or financial power may be useful are allowed in. The Japanese have always seen foreigners as potential pollutants. Even today, when some have travelled or even been trained in Europe or the US, a survey conducted through the Prime Minister's Office indicates that 64 percent of Japanese prefer not to have dealings with foreigners. As for refugees, prior to May 1981, only 853 persons had obtained the right to reside. However, this quota has since risen to 3,000.

4. A 'black hole': everything goes in, but nothing comes out

In astrophysics, a 'black hole' represents an imploding star. Its energy and force of gravity become so dense that it drags in all that comes within reach and allows nothing out, not even light.

An eminent Japanese scholar, professor Tadao Umesao, has observed that Japan behaves like a 'black hole' which absorbs with incommensurable energy whatever comes near it, while nothing

8. Professor K. Murakami, Director of the *Gene Experimental Centre* at the University of Tsukuba, which specializes in research into the manipulation of DNA and other genetic material. The implications of this research are potentially worrying.

9. Doctor Hamao Umezawa, Director of the Institute of Microbial Chemistry. The leading personality in Japan in the field of Biotechnology research and application.

whatever emerges from its abyssal depths.* An example: in the area of science, Japan was, in 1984, the second most productive nation in the world. Between 1978 and 1983, 600,000 articles of a technical or scientific nature were listed in the bibliographies published by the Tokyo National Library. Less than 2 percent of this information has been translated into a western language. This lack of information on Japanese companies is a well-known fact. Apart from such information as the Japanese are willing to divulge, the substance (production, true quantity of business, marketing, management) largely remains secret. All in all, it is very difficult to bribe any Japanese to obtain any sort of information. Even where information has been published and is available to the public, a Japanese will, as far as he can, elude questions in this area. On the other hand, the Japanese themselves seem quite well informed on their own businesses. A comparative test of five large firms in Germany and Japan produced the following result:

* Tadao Umesao, *Le Japon à l'ère planétaire.*

56 percent of Japanese employees considered themselves well-informed about their company, contrasting with only 7 percent in Germany.

If the Japanese know practically everything about our companies, our lack of information about Japanese firms is well known. I have met numerous managing directors of big Japanese companies, in particular companies specializing in biotechnology. Their welcome is always most cordial. But what they tell you is virtually identical to what is written in their advertising catalogues. Of course no company wants to give away its secrets, but the Japanese are so secretive that even the most banal information is given out parsimoniously. The fundamental rule is to know everything about one's potential rivals, including the Japanese ones, and never let anything out about one's own situation. How many telexes and items of information do western observers in Japan send to their respective countries? How many of them know how to read and speak Japanese? A tiny minority, compared to the Japanese executives and chiefs who know English, French, Italian or Spanish. Moreover, actually to speak and understand Japanese fluently provokes great resentment. And that can sometimes lead to suspicion followed by aggression and rejection. By contrast, as soon as a piece of information seems interesting for the Japanese, it will be translated if necessary and published with an astonishing rapidity.

In the course of the colloqium *Understanding Japan* organized by Jean-Louis Servan-Schreiber, Mr. Machozot, a member of the Economic and Social Council, gave a small personal example. Although he was himself the author of a report on the economic relations of France with Japan, published by the Economic Council, Mr. Machozot had the greatest difficulty in getting hold of 300 copies to give out to his colleagues, friends and patrons in France. A fortnight later, in Japan, he happened to go to a reception. A few friends congratulated him on the excellence of his report. He was astounded to discover that the Japanese had already translated and published this report as a little paperback handbook and distributed several thousand copies of it.

The Japanese take a long-term view of every situation. They habitually think in terms of ten-year projects, and such planning has important consequences:

1. They are taking possession of the greater part of the dollars available in the US, Europe, Africa, and Asia—so as to build up a financial citadel while achieving economic colonization on the quiet.

2. The Japanese have access in Asia to an enormous reservoir of labour, 200 million strong, in addition to the 119 million inhabitants of their own country. This formidable army of workers allows the attainment of colossal plus-values and an increase in the competitiveness of markets.

3. The Western system, both in Europe and the US, is in crisis, and is slowly disintegrating. The Japanese simply step in at the right moment to invest in crisis-torn companies, picking up the best bargains.

4. Foreseeing a predictable protectionism, the Japanese have various contingency plans: they establish their industries in crisis-torn countries, they preserve or create jobs and 'nipponise' countries economically and culturally.

5. The Japanese commercial surplus goes on increasing. Japan will accomplish her enormous leap forward into the technologies of the future. She has every chance of becoming the world's leading power in ten years.

6. The victorious arrogance of the Japanese could bring about her rejection in various situations. On the other hand the West could be led to question itself about what it is that gives Japanese dynamism its peculiar quality, and to exploit that.

5. Attack and defence

On Sunday, 7 December 1941, 360 Japanese aeroplanes took off from six aircraft-carriers 275 nautical miles from Hawaii. In a few hours, after a surprise assault that has gone down in history, they had destroyed 90 percent of the American Pacific fleet: this was the famous Pearl Harbour attack, launched by Admiral Yamomoto Isoroku, Commander-in-Chief of the Japanese fleet, with the agreement of the whole of the general staff. Japan and the US were still at peace, and at that very moment negotiations were going on in Washington to try and avoid war. But Yamamoto, fearful of his ability to defeat the Americans if it came to war, wanted to terrorize them with one hammer-blow. The US and the whole world were indeed astounded, but as far as the Americans were concerned, the strategy of the hammer-blow achieved precisely the opposite effect, uniting American public opinion in favour of war. Perhaps that is what Roosevelt wanted, since he knew about the attack 24 hours in advance, but did not inform the commandant at Hawaii. As is well known, he led his country to victory over Japan.

This strategy of inflicting death blows out-of-the-blue has been a characteristic feature of Japan throughout her long history. The rule is that once an action has been decided on there must not be a hairs breadth between attack and defence. It is the secret of any battle and a fundamental rule in the martial arts. At the time of the war of the clans, every strong chief always began his attack with an unexpected strike, which had been meticulously prepared. When the moment for action has come, that action has to be powerfully destructive.

On the night of 8/9 February 1905, Admiral Togo made a similar attack on the Russian base at Port Arthur before there had even been an official declaration of war. Tōgō immobilized and destroyed a great part of the fleet before the Russians, like the Americans later at Pearl Harbour, had a chance to realize what was happening to them. He immobilized the great Russian vessels by sinking one of his own boats in the harbour entrance. Again, on 27 May 1905, Togo intercepted the Russian Baltic Fleet in the Narrows of Tsushima. It was the greatest and most modern fleet of the day. This was a further surprise attack planned with incredibly minute attention to detail. The strategy of this battle is one of the most perfect ever seen in the history of great navies. Only two or three boats escaped from the disaster. In one night, Japan became one of the world's greatest maritime powers. For the first time in history, an Asiatic country had managed to beat a Western power. For the first time too, a great hope began to grow in the Asiatic nations, for whom the preponderance of the West thenceforth ceased to be an absolute myth.

In the thirties, Admiral Suetsugu gave another good definition of strategy that is also a key to all the martial arts: 'The secret of success in battle is to remember that there is no line of demarcation between attack and defence.' The secret consists in being always ready. The more hidden the power, the stronger it is. One must never declare or show one's force. When one attacks, the blow must be faultless and unexpected. Whether in war or economics, the bolt-from-the-blue' is the basis of all Japanese strategy.

The samurai trained themselves to remain alert even while they were asleep. Whatever their posture, whether they were lying down, seated, or having tea, invariably their right hand could almost instantaneously seize their sword and hit out. Consequently the art

10. Swordmaster Kuroda Hichitaro (Seventh dan) in the garden of the Meiji
    sanctuary in Tokyo. The art of drawing the sword (iai) to understand
    self-mastery is applied to spontaneous lightning attack.

of drawing the sword (or *iai*) became a secret art, even though it was
taught in numerous schools. Unless they are overwhelmed by some
immense catastrophe, the Japanese leaders will always remain wedded
to this strategy, which knows how to wait for the moment to act
with lightning suddenness.

6. Hierarchy: one heart, one body

Today the Japanese continue to venerate their emperor as if he were
still sacred. His disappearance would be inconceivable and without
him Japan would no longer be the same, indeed perhaps would even
cease to exist. For Japan is the only country in the world where the
imperial dynasty has continued in being without a break from the
days of its mythical origin 2000 years ago until now. All the Japanese,
descending from the primordial couple *Izanagi-Izanami*, are members
of one and the same family through their emperor. Furthermore, the
Emperor is the chief priest of the original religion, Shinto. He is still
the keystone, the one who determines the totality of Japanese reality

whether political, economic, or religious. At a time of crisis, his voice will be decisive and preponderant above all the parties. No Japanese, whatever his situation and power, could go against his decision. Although the first article of the Constitution states that the emperor is no longer anything more than 'the symbol of the State and of the unity of the people' and that he owes 'his functions to the will of the people in whom resides the sovereign power', he continues to incarnate the overall visible and invisible strategy of Japan. It is through him that the land of Japan is sacred, that she is 'the land of the gods' of whom he is still the representative and the direct descendant. He is without doubt the 'father' of the nation, and it is precisely on this paternalist conception, on this absolute hierarchic verticality that the whole structure of the nation rests.

Such continuity means that Japan is, as we have said, one huge ideal family, with the emperor as its father and guardian. He is above the law. He is himself the Law. It is true that the Emperor's powers are

11. Emperor Hirohito, the Chief Shinto priest, followed by his wife on a visit to the Shinto sanctuary of Shimonoseki. The persistence of a tradition in which the emperor is always the king-priest of a goddess: Amaterasu, the chief *kami* of Japan, goddess of the Sun.

attributed by the New Constitution to the people, but this does not have much meaning for the Japanese. The indomitable and fundamental power of modern Japan lies unquestionably in the ineradicable respect and veneration the people continue to have for their emperor. It is impossible to overstress a concept that is so fundamental for understanding Japanese history, a keystone that is so decisive in structuring the totality of Japanese reality, whether religious, political, philosophical or economic. Every strategy has both a visible and an invisible side. The emperor incarnates these two sides in himself alone. It would be wrong to underestimate the importance of this fundamental reality by seeing in the existence of the emperor nothing more than the symbolic permanence of an ancestral situation.

If it is true then, that the emperor symbolizes the apex of the pyramid, it is also true that hierarchy permeates every level of Japanese society. The *Meiji* restoration of 1868 merely transposed to the economic and political domains the model inherited from the clans. The clans were ruled by a lord, and today he is the managing director of the company. The lord had around him an inner circle of high-ranking intimates (*jūyaku*). These are nowadays the senior executives. Under them were the samurai, who represent the other ranks of the executives. Finally, the mass of employees correspond to the ordinary soldiers. Despite appearances, the feudal structure of business is not in fact *dirigiste* in the narrow sense. Of course all the power is in the hands of the boss/lord, but more than anything else, being in charge means getting the agreement of senior or middle-ranking executives and sometimes even of the workers. On the way to realization, a project moves downwards from the upper ranks to the lower and then has to move up again, with or without modifications, from the base. This process frequently leaves it the richer, and it is what in practice forms the famous Japanese 'consensus'.

The basis of this consensus is the unconditional fidelity that the employee accords his bosses, together with his complete self-identification with the business, which thereby becomes more important than his own family group. Rights and duties are reciprocal. In the old days, the lord looked after his suzerains and vassals. Similarly today, the boss of a large company very frequently behaves like a father when it comes to the major events in the lives of his employees, such as marriages, births, and deaths. Finally, the feudal spirit is also reflected in salary structures, which are related to length of service. Thus the

Japanese dynamic emerges from highly complex structures, structures at once supple and rigid and always incomprehensible to the foreigner.

There is always then, a prior consensus, tacit but national, behind every decision made by a politician or by a businessman. All union disputes are secondary to this consensus. Every decision totally commits the person who takes it. Japanese strategy is incomprehensible without a grasp of this ethic of co-responsibility. It may be true that the way of life of people in business or politics is very close to that in the West, but all the time this co-responsibility (one for all and all for one) with its attendant respect for an underlying hierarchy, is there underneath.

With us in the West, individualism is not only the motor of our expansion but also the principle that causes our failures. In Japan, individualism means that superiority depends on recognition by the group. This sets apart the 'master', the *sensei*, who enjoys considerable respect. It does not matter whether he is immensely rich, like Kōnosuke Matsushita, or from the poorer classes—a potter or a master archer—a *sensei* remains a man of wisdom and a source of instruction. He is equally respected and listened to. Yet there is no-one who is less conformist than the Japanese *sensei*. Indeed, he is the most paradoxical of beings. But character and behaviour traits that would be extremely shocking in others are in him regarded as marks of wisdom. In some places, he is above the law.

Western individualism is an epidermal disease of endless recrimination in the name of the particular interests of individuals and their strict corporate defence. All particular interests are opposed *en bloc* to the general interest. As a corollary we find a profound mis-understanding of the individual and his real qualities, and also of his potential for advancement. It is a merciless battle of the deaf, and often the weaker are crushed by the stronger. Japanese conformism is in its essence prodigiously non-conformist, whereas Western non-conformism generates a stifling bourgeois conformism. Clan warfare in Japan is a serious matter, but it resolves itself in the common interest, whereas in the West clan struggles are to the bitter end, even if that means the destruction of State and society in toto.

The media picture of Japan is of an ageing tiger, weakened in every sphere by an explosion of western consumption. Despite appearances, every manifestation of iconoclasm in Japan is strictly controlled. 'Making money' by all possible means seems to be the sole concern of the nation. And the crucible of competition prevails

there as much as elsewhere. but the crucial thing is that everything
is allowed only within the framework of a conformism that never
threatens any of the implicit laws of the nation: hierarchy, the sense

12. A demonstration in the Akasaka district of Tokyo. In Japan, going on
strike means putting an armband on . . . but continuing to work.
Demonstrations are authorized . . . as long as they stop at traffic lights
and do not impede the traffic.

of duty, the work ethic and the respect for 'custom'. In fact, the Press and television alike respect this rule. They entertain and inform without ever questioning the values of the hierarchy, the sense of collectivity, and the different rules of respect that arise from this. Intellectuals are marginalized or accepted to the extent that they do not confuse individualism with liberalism. The creative person who in one way or another respects accepted values even while he adapts them has his plane in Japan. The others are at liberty to leave. All dissension, once expressed, can be deadened like a powerful wave that washes into the sand. Extreme dissidence that cannot be harnessed is crushed pitilessly. Japanese solidarity in the face of the foreigner is monolithic. Even when scandals are known to all, the Japanese retains his reserve about them in the face of the foreigner. This is a nation that prefers to wash dirty linen within the family.

Inside every company and even within the State there is always some eminent person who has no real power, but whose function is to take a detached view of everything. He is a kind of invisible eye of judgement, equity and wisdom, even if this is a wisdom directed primarily towards the interest of the company. He is there to be at the helm and maintain continuity through thick and thin. On the surface, internecine battles look as bloody in Japan as anywhere else, but when necessary, everything quickly calms down. Extremism is neither accepted nor even tolerated in Japan. It is crushed mercilessly when it is deficient in wisdom. Whether on the extreme right or on the extreme left, the conventions must at all costs be observed. Big errors may be committed, but the manner of them is all-important. Ultimately the interest of the company prevails over that of the individual.

Relationships between bosses and employees in Japan are based on a concept of loyalty. No one can be forced to show loyalty to a company where there is no counter-balancing factor in the form of a mutual sense of responsibility between boss and employee. Neither of them is there to do injury to the other. Western companies frequently function on the absurd principle of divide and rule, with no holds barred. The result is that at a visceral level there is always a latent readiness to rebel against the boss, and a context of conflictual relationships that keep in business hordes of lawyers and their clerks. In Japan there are 70 to 80 percent less court cases than in most of the Western countries. We belong to a sick society, and indeed to a society that is in one sense deeply dishonest, for the weaker goes to the wall. This may be a very unpleasant truth, and fortunately as a general rule it admits of numerous exceptions, but nonetheless it needs to be stated. On such a foundation of moving sand the West is of course totally unable to base any strategy. There is nothing to lean on, no security, no second line of defence for times of crisis. The nature of our 'decline' is evident in the growth of our deficits, in the state of our balance of payments, and in our increasing unemployment. The Japanese are waiting in the wings to take advantage of our weakness and exploit it remorselessly. They are a silent tide that will, it is to be feared, sweep us into economic slavery: they will become our economic masters if not our gurus, and the provisional supremacy of the West will be finished and done with for good.

7. *Between Capitalism and Marxism: Nipponization—a third force*

Perhaps the rise of Japan will be the great event of the twentieth century. Religious patriotism took her close to extinction between 1904 and 1945. But the economic take-off begun in 1950 will make her the foremost world power by the year 2000. Maybe the samurai businessmen will succeed where the militarist samurai failed. Different eras and different methods, but the goal remains the same—world supremacy.

'There is no unity among the nations of the world . . . These rivalries will never cease until someone with an extraordinary power assumes a hegemony and unites all other nations under his sole authority. Among the leaders of the nations there is no-one outside Japan noble or diligent enough to give commands to the whole universe . . . Before the Western nations can be unified under such a leader, it is necessary for us to establish relations, to form alliances, to conclude treaties . . . With our prestige and position assured in this way, the nations of the world will come to regard our Emperor as the great chief of all nations, they will follow our policies and submit to our judgements.'

The author of this quotation was Baron Hotta, who wrote the words in 1858, even before the overthrow of the Tokugawa. They are the more remarkable in that Japan had opened her doors to the West only four years before. From that time, the struggle to attain to hegemony over all the nations of the world has never ceased. No

13. The symbol of the Sun goddess, Amaterasu, has become that of the Emperor and his country. The man who has the power of the sun can rule the world.

Japanese would admit to holding such opinions today, but they remain highly significant.

Japanese strategy has remained and always will remain inflexible in its essence. By definition, the Japanese mind is perfectly ready to pursue a very long-term strategy where necessary. Japan's economic power is always a long-term investment, and there is always a readiness on their part to redraw their plans and make such quick tactical adjustments as may be required. In the protectionist war that has been waged for more than 20 years by Japan against the US and Europe, it is Japan that has practically always been triumphant and Japan that has unfailingly refused to lower the tariff barriers on home territory. In general the free market system functions in only one direction, and the Japanese are impressively skilful at lightening the boat when international tensions are too acute, allowing a few minor inroads into their markets; equally, they are sometimes prepared to do a little sabre-rattling themselves and threaten to put a halt to investments abroad—as they did to the US in December, 1982.

Encirclement tactics are important in the game of *go*, which is a national Japanese game. To get round protectionist legislation the

Japanese have invested massively in the West; more than 20,000 companies have been created, and every year the Japanese set up new records for foreign investment ($5.3 thousand million for the year 1981–82). For the fiscal year 1983, the Japanese had a surplus of $24.28 thousand million, and the surplus in their trade balance increased to $34.6 thousand million from $20.14 thousand million in 1982. The paradise of the Japanese financiers produces the hell of unemployment in the West. But according to *go* strategy, the opponent should not be crushed at the moment when everything is in a bad way. While the game of draughts, which seems vulgar to the Japanese, involves the killing of the king, the game of *go* involves a relative victory. It is sufficient for one side to be the better and to give the other a harsh lesson.

The encirclement of the Italian market provides an excellent illustration and would furnish a wealth of material for a thesis on Japanese strategy. In Milan, where two-thirds of the Japanese resident in Italy are to be found, everything is extremely low-key. The agencies consist only of offices for representatives. But these very men pushed through the Alfa-Nissan agreement with astounding determination in the teeth of the whole Italian bureaucracy. It is a model of its kind. And all the time cars, motorcycles, cameras, typewriters and hi-fi sets are flooding the Italian market to the delight of consumers, who are more than satisfied with their combination of high quality and low prices. But the Italian trade deficit vis-à-vis Japan has reached astronomical levels.

Thus the Japanese strengthen their own position while weakening the economies of other nations. Their next gambit is to invest in a country themselves, thereby helping to restore its economy. Whatever happens, they hold the whip-hand, and this is the most fascinating aspect of the subject. The Japanese are not simply Machiavellian strategists. They are convinced that their management principles can be effective in restoring the whole of the Western economy, especially if the major part of it falls under their control. Their business philosophy is about changing men, it is not simply about improving quality and producing more and better goods; they want to change the conditions of life and ultimately society itself, while raising standards of living. There is a long way to go before all the inhabitants of the planet become consumer-producers, or before terrestrial technology colonizes and conquers space. The Japanese theo-democratic model is an encouragement to all nations to rediscover the deep springs of their own traditions. There has never been a catechism for Confucian indoctrination in Nipponization, but its principles have long been established. We must surely acknowledge that Japanese efficiency and quality manage to perform miracles even in the West. Their greatest and most remarkable success is to have exported not merely their products but even their methods, which are themselves imbued with an underlying ideology. The Japanese third force operates on the principles of the game of *go* or of the martial arts: advance always depends on the selection of a central point on which to bear. The incredible network of production and trade structures organized by the Japanese has an infinite number of centres or points of inter-connection, all linked to one ultimate centre which is the traditional nationalist force of Japan, itself incarnated in the emperor.

Of course the Japanese are quite aware that they cannot export the myth of super-Japan as it is without adapting to differing countries and circumstances. But they have in a sense taken charge of our planetary destiny for the year 2000, by speeding up the pace of historical change, if that were possible. And since the US and the European nations are far from being in a technological Middle Ages themselves, they must face up to the necessity for very painful reconversions. It is fair to ask whether this obvious struggle does not conceal some desperate hopefulness. The Japanese were really terrified when in February 1983, the President of the Council in the USSR, Mr Tikhonov took it upon himself to remind a Japanese business delegation that it would take the Russians just 20 minutes to reduce the 'unsinkable aircraft-carrier' Mr Nakasone was so proud of to molten glass. Is all the dynamic of Japan once again to be needed to save the 'land of the gods' from some potential aggressor? Is the Japanese third force a long-term means of destabilizing the Soviet regime and giving the world a new peace? It is hard to choose between Utopia, realism and nightmare. As for us, we can either wonder, fear or dream.

The heart of the samurai spirit is the preservation of the feeling that the Japanese are a race 'protected by the gods'. As 'sons of Heaven', the Japanese are naturally superior. The only way to knit a company firmly together, the only way to weld a nation is to make each Japanese feel that no matter what the problems may be he can be proud to be first and foremost a Japanese, a being who possesses within himself a part of a sacred heritage. In this sense, Japan is the depository of divine mission. It is true that from her very beginnings, Japan was known as the country of *Wa*, that is to say the country of peace. It is also true that up to the twelfth century Japan offered the spectacle of the most pacific and exquisite of civilizations. But it was precisely the seizure of power by warriors who had previously been the guardians of the nobility, and the emergence of the first strong man in Japanese history, in the person of the Shogun Yoritomo, that signalled radical change in the twelfth century. From then on the philosophy of the samurai was very solidly implanted and defended by a privileged class which still controls politics and business after eight centuries. 'Conquer or die!' is a slogan that seems out of date today, but the Japanese are ultimately ready to sacrifice themselves individually if the higher interests of the nation call for them to do so.

In the thirties, the most westernized of the politicians of the day, Matsuoka Yōsuke (1880–1946) expressed this admirably. 'The mission of the Yamato (Japanese) race is to prevent humanity from becoming devilish, to save it from destruction and to lead it towards the world of light [. . .] Providence is calling on Japan to undertake the mission of delivering humanity from the impasse of modern material civilization.' (*Seiji, Keisai* and *Giho* Reviews, 1933–34.)

This was precisely the thesis of the militarist Tōjō government during the Second World War. Although this messianic type of thought now seems to have been discredited among the Japanese people themselves, the same cannot be said for their leaders. It is worthwhile comparing the credo of the old militarist leaders with Japanese economic expansionism as we know it today. We could summarize thus:

1. The origin of the Japanese race is divine.
2. Japan is the only country in the world where this divine authority continues to be manifest after 2000 years in the person of the emperor.
3. This state of affairs gives Japan a unique supremacy over all other nations.
4. This supremacy must be made manifest on a planetary scale for the good of all humanity.
5. The materialist civilization of the West and all the types of regime that stem from it constitute the contrary of all true civilization, and consequently all the nations which share in this materialistic spirit will inevitably reach an impasse and collapse.

6. Japan is not afraid of Western civilization, whatever the price she may have to pay. The super-Westernization of Japan consists in using the enemy's weapons to beat him all the more convincingly.

7. All that Japan wants is to attain to an irresistible world supremacy in order to give the materialistic nations a lesson in civilization.

No originality of thought is required to discern the following:

1. Japan has replaced military power with economic mobilization.

2. Her strategy in the economic domain is more suggestive of economic warfare than of normal industrial expansion.

3. At least until a recent date, there has existed a state of conflict between the 'pure and hard' policy of a large number of leading figures in Japan and the Japanese people themselves, who are increasingly inclined to balk at the iron fist.

4. Despite appearances, the militarist party has never been out of power. It is they who have achieved the phenomenal success of Japan and they whose art has welded the Japanese into an iron fist, so that each individual feels committed and in total solidarity with the economic struggle. In this sense, they have so far not put a foot wrong.

5. There are a number of plans to cope with the moral disarmament which is becoming evident and which could in the medium term threaten economic expansion itself.

6. Coping with this disarmament means giving back to the nation her sense of sacred cohesion. Thus there is in existence a plan for constitutional reform involving an increase in the powers of the emperor. Young schoolchildren must learn about the heroic leaders who have incarnated Japanese militarism, and in particular Admiral Tōgō.

In 1982, the Ministry of Education aroused furious protests from the Chinese when they had the schoolbooks rewritten. The effect of the changes was to embellish the militarist past and play down its negative aspects. In an interview in *Sankei Shimbun* in August 1981, Tanaka Kakuei, a former Prime Minister, when asked about what he thought of the war against the Chinese and the 11 million Chinese killed, had nothing to say except that he found it 'very regrettable'.

The question which divides Japan most profoundly is this: How to win the economic war without resorting once more to rearmament? How to resist American pressure with its call for more muscle to be given to the Nippo-American security agreement in the shape of renewed Japanese expenditure on armament, increased technological collaboration for military purposes, and the resurgence of a tough and strong Japan that would enable the Americans to have some relief from the weight of their own defensive umbrella? The Japanese are well aware that any commitment in this direction is a grave source of irritation in the Soviet Union and worries Asian countries such as China, Korea, the Philippines, etc., who have no desire to see a restoration of Nippon hegemony as in the heyday of the militarist regime.

Even though they remain committed to the Western camp, the Japanese badly want to preserve peace, and they also want to keep some kind of neutral ground between the two superpowers. Is it Utopian to imagine that Japan could become the Switzerland of Asia? A refuge for international capital and an economic force so powerful that everyone, even the Russians, would be very careful how they handled her.

In January 1983, Nakasone Yasuhiro, Prime Minister of the day, friend and protege of Tanaka, caused an enormous outcry by declaring that in the face of the Soviet threat 'the whole archipelago would have to be like an unsinkable aircraft-carrier, constituting an enormous barricade against the Soviets.' In January 1984, he decided to increase military expenditure by 6.5 percent, so that it now stands at $12.5 thousand million, or 0.991 percent of the gross national product. Within a year, a new series of measures had helped to accentuate the militarist character of Japan and her alignment with the US: a reinforcement of Japan's operational capacities, the launching of her first submarine armed with anti-surface vessel missiles, the *Nadashio*, a vessel of 2,250 tonnes; and there was also the construction by the Mitsubishi, Kawasaki, and Toshiba consortium of a whole new generation of missiles, the bringing to military readiness of new armaments systems, and the reinforcement of telecommunications, munition stocks etc.

There is increased military cooperation with the United States. Military technology is exported to the USA in the domains in which the Japanese are world leaders: these are shrouded in secrecy, but they include radar systems, integrated circuits, optical fibres and electronic equipment. Several big companies, Nippon Electric, Mitsubishi and Hitachi among them, are developing new sectors solely devoted to national defence and armaments. Thus the reinforcement of the means of 'self-defence' is well under way, and cooperation with the US has become even closer. In February 1984, Japan's naval and aero-naval forces joined with the Americans in manoeuvres off the island of Shikoku, baptised *Team Spirit '84*. Japanese bases used by the US are more and more frequently visited by USA warships carrying nuclear weapons. All this is hardly compatible with the 'pacifist' nature of the Constitution.

The Japanese fleet is already sizeable (15 or so submarines and about 50 heavy vessels comprising escorts and frigates equipped with ultramodern aids) and it will soon be expanded. So will the credits assigned for military research and development. Of course, these credits are still relatively low in relation to the GNP (1 percent). But there is every likelihood that the present tendency will become ever stronger. The important thing to remember is that the Nakasone government has committed itself to cooperation in the maintenance of a Western defence front.

Discreet though it may be, the new militarist strategy of Japan is naturally unwelcome to the Kremlin and brings back bad memories to the other Asiatic countries. But the choice seems irreversible despite strong resistance from within Japan. The strategy of the strong man in a strong country also aims at a new ideological and military mobilization of the nation, at the very moment when the new generation in Japan would finally like to enjoy some well-being after so many years of expansion.

8. The quiet revolution

When the all-powerful *MITI* announced in 1981 the initiation of research into the 'fifth generation computer', to be operational by 1990 or 1991, international experts could not conceal their astonishment. Once again, Japan was banking on the improbable and forcing the US and the Europeans to rush into the fray too or risk finding themselves suddenly left behind in the race to the future.

This superproject involves devising an 'intelligent' computer able to reason, and capable not simply of acquiring information and memorizing it, but actually of gaining some kind of experience from it, and even of expressing itself with human sounds. This concept no longer belongs in the realm of science fiction, now that it is starting to take concrete shape under the aegis of ICOT (Japanese Institute for new generation Computers), provided with a budget of 11 million dollars for 1983 and a team of 50 information engineers under the direction of Professor Fuchi Kazuhiro. All the members of the team are under 35. All the leading companies, like Fujitsu, NEC, Hitachi, Mitsubishi, Toshiba, Oki, Matsushita and Sharp, have contributed their top brains. Global investment in the project is estimated at $426 million.

This challenge illustrates the dynamism and near-supremacy of the Japanese electronics industry. The Americans are particularly worried. Now the Japanese possess their own Silicon Valley, which they have established in Kyushu and baptised appropriately 'Silicon Island'. Not only that, but Japanese involvement in the real Silicon Valley continues to grow. In 1983, Japanese exports of integrated circuits to the United States were worth $750 million, aggravating the American deficit in this sector by the outflow of $320 million.

Of course, there is no certainty that the Japanese will necessarily win the battle of the brains, and there is danger in awakening the American giant. However, in throwing all their weight into research, the Japanese are setting a challenge for themselves. The directors of *MITI* know that unless they are first, there is no salvation for Japan—if she wants to retain the mastery of South-East Asia, where competition is every bit as harsh, a new Japan must be invented. Hence a colossal battle rages in every sphere: optical fibres and the transmission of information by laser, robotics, reinforced ceramics, and also the life sciences, genetics, and biotechnology.

In the battle for space, Japan also wants to show her independence, although she is still a long way behind the US, the USSR and Europe. But since 1970 the Japanese have launched about 30 satellites of a scientific or commercial nature. Here too they are putting on a spurt. But the thrust of the Japanese efforts is going into cryogenic propulsion, the propulsion that enables the space shuttle to fly, and they intend to equip a rocket with a motor having a ten tonne thrust, slightly superior to that of the Ariane rocket. Will this samurai strategy carry them along too fast and too far?

Whether she likes it or not, Japan is condemned to become the world's leading nation economically; she must win the battle of the future or she will disappear. But the excessive power of Japan actually rests on an excessive weakness: that of a really rather small territory, hardly any larger than Italy, where the population density has risen in the last hundred years from 90 to 316 per square metre. Today Japan has 119 million inhabitants, and there will be 130 million by the year 2000. She imports about 50 percent of her food requirements and even now almost the whole of her energy and raw materials. Moreover, life-expectation has gone from 47 years at the beginning of the century to an average of 74 years for men and 79 for women. Ultimately, the ageing of executives and employees is likely to threaten the structure of the businesses themselves, since they are based on lifetime employment and the progression of salaries. On the other hand, the newer generations are much less well motivated to sacrifice themselves constantly in the name of the nation's future grandeur. All the more so in that out of 58 million workers, only 20 percent are the privileged employees of the big companies, which effectively take charge of their personnel and preserve jobs even in times of crisis. The great majority of Japanese work in the PMEs, the sub-contracting sector, where they earn 20 percent less and lack any social or work security. But there is the same moral commitment and sense of coresponsibility in the two cases, not least because it is the PMEs that are the first to suffer at times of crisis.

Up to now, a sentiment that is both nationalist and religious has bonded Japanese society and made the Japanese accept the greatest sacrifices. From as far back as 1854, when the six black warships of Commodore Perry and his 600 white barbarians made the Japanese realize that the 'land of the gods' could be conquered, Japan has been perpetually mobilized and in a state of frequently near-heroic tension, striving to appropriate the weapons and structures of her rivals in her determination to dominate them.

In the thick of economic competition, Japan is today threatened by the protectionist measures of the West, by the vigorous competitiveness of countries like South Korea, Taiwan, Singapore and Hong Kong, by the new *Chinese economic mobilization* in the medium term and finally by the proximity of the USSR, an old enemy whose missiles are profoundly worrying.

Whether it be militaristic or economic in character, Japan's mobilization cannot therefore lose its eternally 'hard and pure' nature. What matters is not some myth of a super-Japan, but rather the absolute necessity for the country to develop a strategy that is both internal and international, a strategy that will maintain national cohesion and national supremacy at any price.

Japanese democracy will never be Western democracy as long as Japan is set on this course. That is why an elite 'club' with less than 3000 members, including politicians, civil servants, bankers and businessmen, directs the destinies of 119 million Japanese. The whole Japanese strategy depends on the uncompromising dynamic of 'conquer or die'. This idea may seem over-stated, when put so nakedly, but it definitely conveys the fundamental situation of a country where love for cherry blossoms, reflecting the impermanence of everything, symbolizes a sensibility which makes a cult of the indefinable and yet at the same time accepts that the union of life and death is but one single whole.

Today the Japanese militaristic philosophy of 'conquer or die' has veiled its extremist and warlike face and has transformed itself into the 'quiet revolution'. These are the terms employed by Prime Minister Nakasone Yasuhiro when he set out his programme at the hundredth session of the national Parliament on 9 September 1983.

The 'quiet revolution' implies above all the reinforcing of creativity, the encouragement of flexibility and expansion of the Japanese economy at any price. It means developing personal initiative 'in order to make it a more effective and dynamic tool for the revitalization of society and the economy, so as to stimulate evolution towards the twenty-first century.'

This is a lucidly-expressed lesson that our rulers would do well to apply: but here it illustrates the constant process of re-examination to which the Japanese subject all their structures, with the aim of adapting them to the eternal present which is preparing for the future.

Is Japan *dirigiste*? Of course she is, as long as it fits her bill, as long as there is flexibility and a willingness to leap into the driving seat of the near future: for Japan has never been better mobilized than she is today to win this gigantic battle at any price. Her flexibility is a change of direction that consists in adapting inner structures and neutralizing external adversaries: she is putting in all the necessary investment, and adopting all the necessary strategies. Whatever happens, there must be no faint hearts, and the rhythm of expansion must be held or quickened. The partial 'opening-up' of the Japanese market will operate to the advantage of that same market, especially in the high technology sectors.

9. The Japan of the future: action is an eternal present

One of the great strengths of the Japanese outlook resides in its ability to combine long-term planning with a capacity for very rapid rethinking and response when necessity so dictates. Foresight of this kind is related to the 'rhythm' associated with the nature of things, that is to say with human structures and human life. Instantaneous action belongs to the imponderable, non-analyzable nature of reality. The martial arts tradition and economic strategy alike owe their power to an understanding of, and a combination of, both terms.

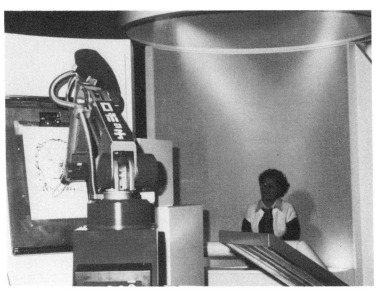

14. Now there is a robot that will draw your portrait. The delicate touch of the robot can today trace out the lines of your face.

It is an unvarying feature of Japanese isolationism that the nation preserves her independence. In the military sense, Japan has never been conquered. Even the Mongol armies that terrorized such a large part of the planet in the thirteenth century, failed twice to seize Japan. The American occupation of 1945 cannot be compared to the conquest of a territory. The Japanese consider that their independence must be preserved at any price and in the face of one and all. It is this that explains the fantastic conversion of Japan from a feudal society to an ultramodern nation in less than 50 years. But precisely this industrial conversion has placed Japan in a condition of considerable economic dependence. And that is her Achilles heel. Japan in fact imports virtually the whole of her energy and raw materials (phosphates, ferrous metals, bauxite, nickel, manganese, chrome and petrol). But she has now got her eyes fixed on the horizon of the year 2000, by which date this vital question will have been largely resolved. A new Japan, the Japan of the future, is being born out of this ambition. And the Japanese have every reason to come out on top. They are busy setting themselves up for success.

In the next ten years, Japan will spend 5,000 million pounds on the development of substitute sources of energy. Funds are invested in research on geothermic energy, solar energy, coal, tidal and wind energy and nuclear energy. As of now, the Japanese produce 12 percent of their electricity from nuclear energy, and 19 power stations are under construction, with plans for 23 in all. Currently, hydroelectric power stations are supplying 19.8 percent of their energy, 18 percent coming from liquid natural gas and 2.6 percent from coal. The objective is to reduce petrol imports to less than 56 percent. This will mean a 30 percent autonomy in energy.

At Nio, by the inland sea of Seto in the West of Japan, one of the biggest solar power stations in the world has been in operation since 1981. In ten years the Japanese are expecting to build solar power stations in space, positioned on a geostationary orbit. By 1992 *MITI* expects to have in operation a solar power station generating ten Megawatts. An ambitious project involves tapping geothermic energy from about 60 active volcanoes in Kyushu. By the year 2000 they could be generating 40 million Megawatts of energy.

The question of raw materials is more complex. The Japanese have established a consortium for the mining of the under-sea nodules. These nodules are little balls three to ten centimetres in diameter which are to be found in their thousands 5000 metres below the sea. They are made up of manganese and iron oxide, nickel, cobalt, copper and molybdenum. The exploitation of such reserves presents enormous difficulties. All the big industrial nations have also established consortiums with a view to their eventual extraction. But where the Japanese are concerned, dreams have a way of becoming reality. The Institute of Space Sciences is planning the construction of a space shuttle 52 metres long and 28 metres wide. Nor is it beyond the bounds of possibility that the Japanese will go and exploit the wealth of minerals on the moon.

10. The strategy of the future

Inventing the future means going well beyond the technological superiority of which Japan is the master. By contrast the USA which has produced innumerable Nobel Prize winners, has quite a lead in the domain of pure research. The invention and discovery of revolutionary principles are above all the product of pure science, but here Japan is appreciably behind. And yet pure research will very probably constitute the basis of twenty-first century industry. The Japanese are aware of this problem and are already striving to achieve a complete transfer of priorities from technology to science. They are currently organizing the means to realize their ambitions.

The big Japanese universities are now giving priority to producing high-level scientists and engineers. On average they currently turn out 800 scientists for every 74,000 engineers. This is far from sufficient, and the Japanese are making every effort to induce scientists all over the world to join their camp and take their side in the competition for the future.

In May 1983, Parliament voted the construction of 19 industrial research centres to be sited at various locations in Japan. These are to be the famous *Technopolis*. The most prestigious of these centres is already in existence, 60 kilometres from Tokyo. It is the *Tsukuba Science City*. It was established in 1963 to be the 'seed of the future', and it brings together about 7,000 scientists, engineers and technicians. Its annual budget is of the order of $600 million. In May 1984, the list of the 14 technology cities which are to be established was published. One of the principal objectives of these is to stimulate university research by linking it more closely to the ultramodern enterprises being established in the *Technopolis*.

PART 2

15. A sketch of Miyamoto Musashi. A million Americans have bought his
     initiatory treatise: *The Book of the Five Rings*. He is a model for the
     understanding of strategy and tactics, and the almost invincible power
     of self-mastery.

2

TACTICS AND STRATEGY IN THE SAMURAI TRADITION

A Western businessman would undoubtedly be amazed to be told that his knowledge of strategy and marketing would be enriched by a wealth of original ideas if he were to acquaint himself with the spirit and tactics of the samurai.

Since samurai principles always underly the thinking of Japanese higher executives and big company managing directors, whose practice embodies them unvaryingly, the tradition is well worth studying. In any sizeable company there will almost certainly be a dōjō for training in martial arts such as karate, jūdō, and kendō, and the boss himself is likely to be seen working out there regularly.

1. Miyamoto Musashi

Miyamoto Musashi (1594–1645), is one of the great legendary figures of Japan about whom, paradoxically, little is known. Nevertheless, literally hundreds of books have been published about him in Japan. Scarcely a week goes by without his adventures being on television or radio. If there is such a thing as a samurai 'western', Miyamoto is certainly its greatest star. He himself would certainly have been most surprised by such fame. His own life is almost a complete mystery to us. The first book about this extraordinary personality did not appear until 100 years after his death. Entitled the *Niten ki*, it is clearly a hagiographical work, a melange of real events and fictitious stories intended chiefly to fire the reader's imagination. The only reliable information in this account consists of certain indisputable facts that are confirmed by other narratives and chronicles.

We know that Miyamoto Musashi, a painter by profession, was a wanderer practically all his life. He went from school to school, from town to town, offering assistance and aid to local lords, sharing his science and his knowledge of battle with an elect few, then setting off again. This perpetual wandering symbolizes a thirst for freedom. The true samurai cannot become attached to any object, not even to life itself. He passes on because the principle of all things resides in movement. It is a way of escaping from the clogging desire to possess: the man on the move takes nothing with him but himself. At the same time, this wandering has another goal: on the road, anything may happen. The samurai is always on the alert. Musashi never hesitated to challenge the masters of the great sword schools all around the country. These schools were by definition secret. The art of the sword was essentially an esoteric art involving initiation. Of course all the samurai knew how to fight, but real masters were few and far between. Musashi had no fear of challenging them. Before the age of 30, he had already fought virtually all the great fights of his career—about thirty in all. His evolution as a great fighter was effectively without parallel. It bears a resemblance to that of the great Japanese artist Hokusai, who despite his extraordinary talent, reckoned that he only began to understand the art of drawing at the age of 40, and hoped he would really get to be able to draw by the time he was 80. Musashi was an equally precocious child. He won his first fight at the age of 13. But all through his life he strove to translate his naturally virtuoso techniques into real wisdom and science. This is what led him to write his famous 'Book of the Five Rings' (Gorin-no-Sho). Musashi ended his days aged 60 in remarkable fashion, like a kind of St. Francis of the sword. He shut himself away in a cave to meditate. Alone with himself in his solitude he set out the precepts of the Way. It was a way for which he had given up everything, a way that he wanted to pass on to his chief disciple.

If Musashi was alive now, he would be astonished to see how his precepts have been used, precepts that were really secrets meant for the edification of a single disciple who was already an unquestioned master. What he wrote was in fact a summary, a guide on the intermediate or advanced level for the use of a samurai who actually already knows and practices this teaching.

The *Book of the Five Rings* has sold more than a million copies. The American publisher exploited the ambiguity of the words 'tactics' and 'strategy' as understood by Masashi, and presented the book as a key to Japanese economic strategy.

There is no doubt that Musashi's rule remains eternally valid: the more one gains mastery over oneself, the more one masters external reality. Granted there is a world of difference between Musashi's ascetic way and the mentality of a modern business chief, nonetheless it is true that if we translate into today's terms we see that it is not unusual to meet business chiefs for whom spiritual values, a sense of self-mastery and even the riches of meditation do have a meaning. While it is true that the majority are notable for their obsessional fixation on the financial profits of their business and on the conquest of markets at any price, there are top bosses who are concerned about having a philosophy of life and who take a lively interest in everything that has to do with an understanding of reality. Thus although there is no simple symmetrical equivalence between Musashi's teaching and the assumptions of a modern business chief, nonetheless the comparison is instructive purely as an analogy.

2. The secret of the Way and the mastery of the centre

Combat is only a way of making apparent something that already exists. That is why Musashi says that a battle is always won before it begins, since it is won in the mind.

The Way is a matter of assuring mastery of the centre. The centre is stability and harmony. It is from the centre that everything moves out and to the centre that everything comes back. In this sense it is the place of all energies. But according to Musashi, 'this place is *empty*'.

How can vacuity determine absolute success? Faced with an adversary armed with a sabre, a warrior confronts an absolute choice: to die or to continue living. And this absolute will be decided in a fraction of a second. For the gesture of cutting is as swift as a bullet. What is it that determines the success or failure of this fraction of a second? If I reply 'the mastery of emptiness', these terms are not as contradictory as they seem.

This thought is in fact the key to all tactics and enables us to comprehend that where traditional masters are concerned there is only actually one teaching. Thus, for example, it is remarkable to what extent the masters of the different arts say precisely the same thing. In the fourteenth and fifteenth centuries, the *doyen* of the Nō theatre was called Zeami. He strove to instil a teaching which would form the whole man on the basis of the Nō theatre. Like Musashi, Zeami wrote a treatise to leave to his foremost disciple, on the understanding that he in turn would hand it on to another.

This treatise, *The Secret Tradition of Nō*, is also, in its way, an essay on tactics, even though it is seemingly written for actors. In it there is the same rule of the centre, which Zeami calls the rule 'of skin, flesh and bones' in the sense that if things are to exist and if art is to be accomplished, a man must be united to himself as the skin is to the flesh and the flesh is to the bones. Some of Zeami's observations about actors are precisely the same as those made by Musashi about the samurai. The actor always wants to overdo it. He acts for the sake of the facade, he makes a spectacle of himself. He does not interiorize his art. Likewise the samurai, according to Musashi, indulge in a great deal of futile histrionics. They are all too prone to leap into the air, jump from side to side, and utter terrifying shrieks, merely in order to make a sword-thrust. Today we would say that they were 'showing off', making a spectacle of themselves. But there are not 36 ways of delivering a sword-thrust, says Musashi: there is only downwards, upwards, from left to right and from right to left. The man who knows these strokes and does them well is a complete swordsman. The great tactic then, is great simplicity. Great simplicity is always the result of great harmony, harmony is the result of presence to oneself and the whole comes from a consciousness that never allows itself to be captured either by distraction or by concentration. Working with what is means integrating all physical, psychical and spiritual qualities and making them as effective and weightless as a.puff of air. This is the price of great art.

The centre can be assimilated to what is. In sudden action, there exists a moment placed between life and death: it is the Instant. The Instant is outside time. It simply is. It is what there is of eternity in man and in all things. The fighter becomes accustomed to living in Instants. In Instants there is no longer life and death. Each confrontation between two samurai is in its own way the art of living that instant. It is the instant in which being and non-being become one in a fraction of a second. There is no more life and death. The sense of wandering and travelling is precisely the sense that man does not come from anywhere and is not going anywhere. He just *is*. And this 'being' is in Musashi's thought taken up and carried to a singular and strange level of perfection: a perfection in which he puts at risk his own life and that of the adversary, not so much for the sake of fighting, but rather for the sake of the challenge to realize this perfection, this perfect and absolute confrontation with the Instant.

Here I would like to tell a story that illustrates the extent to which extremes are separated by nothing more than a hairs breadth.

A shogun (prime minister in feudal Japan) heard tell of a great Zen master who accomplished prodigies and possessed universal knowledge. So he decided to meet him. 'What is hell and what is paradise?' he asked him. The Zen monk looked at him and suddenly started to shower him with insults. The shogun listened imperturbably to the abuse, until the insults became increasingly precise and offensive and he lost his temper: suddenly he drew his sword from its scabbard and advanced threateningly towards the monk who began to retreat towards the wall, continuing to pour out abuse. When the monk stopped, the shogun, beside himself, raised his arm to strike. At this point the monk grabbed his elbow and shouted: 'That's what hell is.' The shogun hesitated a moment and then let his arm drop. The monk shouted: 'That's what paradise is.'

True tactics dispense with tactics. Between life and death there is a link. This link is the Whole. It is the elusive freedom of being. It is the endless activity of the centre, which probably has no other final purpose than this activity itself.

3. Being sure of the depths

It must be understood that when Musashi tells us that we must 'be sure of the depths' he means by this that every being possesses depths to which he must gain access. All knowledge and all energy preexist in us. It is our job to find out the extent to which they are similar, indeed identical to the very forces of the Universe. The 'depths' are the knowing in which everything coincides. In this sense, it is because man is free that movement arises spontaneously and that efficiency is acquired too. Tactics enable the form and the foundation to reveal themselves and potentialize one another.

The 'depths' indispensable for all success are learned by meditation, by work, and by a rigorous way of life. The fighter understands how energies operate and how the centre integrates them. Or, as we would say, how they express themselves or manifest themselves in the rapid and the slow, the strong and the gentle. The person who does not know always perceives forces as contrary and opposed, the person whose consciousness is awakened sees in contradictory aspects necessary complementarities, dynamic forms which await only conscious mastery to be harmonized and potentialized. Thus a defeat may contain a victory and vice-versa.

The 'depths' also consist of a unitary vision of everything. It is a law of harmony that is found in Japan as in China. If it is not understood, the critic is quick to say that the whole thing is just a matter of words or philosophical concepts which have nothing to do with reality. That is not simply an error, it is an enormous error. For what is at issue is the most analytic and rational process imaginable. A process which is instinctively that of a good many Western chiefs. To undertake an enterprise, to give responsibilities to an individual is a serious matter. By virtue of this 'law of harmony', a Japanese is very quickly able to assess whether your overall qualities are in harmony and whether you are a person upon whom one can rely. While you are talking figures and profits, your interlocutor will be analyzing the quality of the men behind the business. That is why a Japanese will never say why he takes so much time to come to a decision, whether positive or negative. His priority is to make a minutely detailed global analysis of the situation. At the same time there is a process of testing. An infinite number of factors of a seemingly 'irrational' nature will be taken into account. Analyses will be not simply of an economic or psychological character, as one might expect. The philosophy of harmony has as a corollary, what one might call the 'science of interactions'. Interactions are complex but logical processes which flow from a given situation. The overall view of a situation (the 'globalizing' vision) makes it possible to deduce the interactions which flow from it. This is at once analysis and more than analysis. It involves a science which operates on several levels, a science which allows both deduction and induction. All decisions imply a strategy, and this strategy consists not merely in adding up the strong and the weak points but also in considering them relative to the persons and companies involved. A Japanese executive will look behind any piece of business to see the spirit of the enterprise and study the personnel involved in it. The 'accounting exercise', if I may call it that, will consider not simply the past and the present but also the future possibilities. In other words, *that which is made explicit* makes it possible to deduce implicit phenomena which may show up in the future.

4. The duel between Musashi and Gonosuke Musō

Musashi learnt this principle for himself at his own expense. He was beaten only once in his long career, but this was an exemplary defeat that is worth describing. The grand master of the short stick (or jo) was then called Gonosuke Musō. He was an accomplished samurai, versed in the use of all weapons. But he preferred to fight with the short stick, which he handled with inimitable skill. Like Musashi, he travelled all over Japan visiting different schools (or ryu) without ever being defeated. Inevitably the two men's paths had to cross one day. When this happened, they squared up to each other. Musō attacked first, Musashi parried immediately, using his two-sword technique, and put Musō in a dangerous situation. Musashi magnanimously refused to exploit his advantage and spared Musō's life.

This defeat caused Musō immense distress. For a time his despair knew no bounds. He had suffered a defeat he found totally inexplicable. So he retreated to the top of Mount Homan, on the island of Kyūshū and began a life of extreme discipline and severity. In the course of a sleepless night he had a revelation and heard a sentence he did not understand: 'Know the organs with a log'. Then, one day, the meaning of this saying was revealed to him. The word 'log' meant that he must change his tactics and use a short stick. Musō cut one out of the hardest oak he could find and called it jō. He established 12 fundamental movements for jō, and they became the basis for his new teachings, jojutsu. Later he realized that the word 'organ' that occurred in the message was to be interpreted as a way of directing attacks at the enemy's weak points (atemi). The short stick in fact enabled him to get nearer to his adversary. Eventually the day of his revenge arrived, and Musō challenged Musashi. This time the unthinkable happened and it was Musō who emerged victorious. But he followed Musashi's own example in sparing him his life.

This story is a lesson that is always up-to-date. There is in fact no such thing as a master, however great his skill and mastery, who does not one day encounter a master greater than himself. The greatest masters of budō in Japan have had harsh experience of this. Nor are the founders of the great schools any exception to the rule. In other words there are no limits in an art in which pure thought, pure energy and pure movement are but one. It has an important lesson for us too, since all our concepts are based on sizes and quantities, on notions of strength and output; we live reality on the first level or to the first degree. Musashi and Musō, faithful to the spirit of oriental tradition, make use both of positive and negative energy. The point of assault bears on a precise location, or *atemi*, and focuses all the energy on a minute area. This point is a vital one. On it depends life or death. But such focusing on the point of maximum effectiveness is not sufficient. There is the self and the other, and then, at the second degree, there no longer exists either subject or object, or self or the other, but an interaction between them. Musō understood like Musashi that the person who is no longer duality but has become interaction itself, the person who himself inseparably becomes rhythm, force and movement, that person unites positive and negative energy, *yin* and *yang*, the fire principle and the water principle, the earth principle and the heaven principle. This is why quality of consciousness triumphs over number. And it is a reminder of a golden rule—namely, that a true principle always reduces a large or even enormous number to one.

5. Calligraphy, Zen, and the sword

Musashi was undoubtedly better known in his day for his calligraphic talents than for his exploits with the sword. An accomplished artist in the skin of a fine fighter. This is a double-faced reality that scarcely makes sense. Can there be any analogy between the art of making the brush-stroke spring out and the art of making the sword spring out? Let us take this comparison further. The practice of *sumi-e*, at which Musashi excelled, consists of executing a drawing on a piece of very fine silk paper with a single free and instantaneous stroke. This paper has the property of absorbing ink like blotting paper. The brush, on the other hand, is relatively thick and soaked in black ink. The stroke must of necessity be light, aerial, and spontaneous, the movement faultless and immaculate in the literal sense of the word, since the least error is immediately punished by a blot and the drawing wrecked. The art of the sword, like *sumi-e*, becomes the art of touching the limits, of allowing the emergence, not of the action-thought, but of the very breath of the thought, if I can put it like that. It is a question of acting not on the thing but on the soul or spirit of the thing. In fact there is no better way of learning anything than by realizing the endless and bottomless unity of all art, and by acting not with a part but with the whole of one's being, its aerial essence that is both free

16. & 17.   A drawing of a horse and the portrait of a monk (over page) by Miyamoto Musashi. An artist as great with the brush as with the sword.

and anchored, open and centred. No doubt that is why a man as accomplished as Musashi practised calligraphy, which is considered the seventh martial art.

Similarly Zen Buddhism finds in *sumi-e* and calligraphy both illustration and practice of the 'action without thought' which is characteristic of it. The analogy between struggle against oneself and struggle with the piece of paper is an endless source for both practice and reflection. If the indefinable, that which is, though beyond all analysis, in fact restores the depth of reality, then one of the best exercises for bringing to light the nature of the void, conceived as the sole concrete reality, is *sumi-e* or calligraphy. This is especially true insofar as at the level of the particle everything is void, and reality is created purely by interactions. But how to conceive the nature of the void apart from what appears to us as the reality? Our concepts need a frontier, that of our own ideas on the nature of things. We can do good work if we begin from our own resistance. Nothing is harder for a Western mind. When Planck himself, father of quantum physics, discovered that the nature of energies is a double-faced reality, continuous and discontinuous, vectorial and vibratory, he wanted to give up physics entirely. And yet what could he do but accept something that a scientific mind simply could not comprehend! The same is true whether it is the void, Zen, or calligraphy that we are studying.

The Void is encountered only when it suddenly reveals itself as a privation. The spontaneous stroke meets with its own resistance. In the presence of inhibitions and fears, the pure white sheet of paper becomes a battlefield. The big, clumsy brush, soaked with ink, becomes like a sword. An over-stressed stroke is not natural enough and produces a wound. The ink, like blood, is very quick to make an ugly blotch. The successful action, on the other hand, manifests the void, or the real. To carry all resistance to its highest point of resistance and to overcome it effortlessly is the only possible style. It is in extreme situations that the true fighter shows himself. In itself the action is pure when the desire to win or lose no longer has any meaning. The 'depths' are revealed when the necessary 'stroke' is made, with a simple and spontaneous inevitability.

6. Three principles of tactics

1. Reducing many enemies to one
The essence of the Way is mastery of the centre. Musashi says it is

necessary to 'be sure of the depths'. If the centre is assured, the rest will be right too. The rest is the visible form, the tactics. Tactics is the art of bringing the centre-point to bear on a multitude of different points almost simultaneously. In this sense the number of adversaries, however great, can always be reduced to one. There is here a really great secret, and it is nothing less than the secret of the universe itself. A great physicist like Geoffrey Chew will today speak of the sudden Event, that of the particle whose complexity is totally manifest instantaneously and at each and every moment. Another way of understanding the rule consists in determining what pertains to local reality and what is 'global'. Local reality is the place where tactics are operative. It is the space-time that we know, insofar as space-time results both from the movement of all things and from the awareness that we have of things. The union of these two aspects is what gives rise to rhythm. Rhythm in its turn gives that subtle mastery over energy and therefore over the adversary. It is the art of controlling the adversary in his own rhythm. In fact, a swifter, truer rhythm always overcomes a slower one.

2. The art of throwing the enemy off balance

On the occasion of his fight with Sasaki Kojirō, Musashi deliberately arrived late. Boiling with impatience, Sasaki had been waiting for him for almost two hours. When he saw Musashi approaching in his boat, he lost his cool and threw the scabbard of his sword into the sea, right in front of Musashi. 'A man who throws his scabbard about has already lost' remarked Musashi. He had obtained the desired effect, he had thrown the enemy off balance, making him lose his *sang-froid*.

While Musashi was walking up the beach, Sasaki gave him a ferocious blow with his sabre, ripping in two the scarf that Musashi was wearing round his head. Musashi in turn struck out with his *boken*, a wooden sabre he had cut out of an oar on his way to the duel. The blow broke Sasaki's skull. Knowing that Sasaki used a long sabre, Musashi had cut his own wooden sabre to a length a few centimentres longer than Sasaki's. He cheerfully waved to the seconds and went straight back to his boat.

3. Harmonizing the spirit of the five elements

We must not forget that when one has united in oneself the water

18. In this little Shinto sanctuary at Uji jinga, near Shimonoseki, Miyamoto Musashi came to rest before his famous duel with Kojirō Sasaki. The moving simplicity of a historic site unchanged for four centuries.

principle, the earth principle, the fire principle, and the wind principle, and when one has assimilated the essence and the substance of these energies, the ultimate principle that crowns the whole is the Void. When someone undergoes training, he does not learn in pedagogic fashion; rather he experiences in himself how each of the five principles is present, and how he can in practice make manifest each of these energies.

7. Rhythm: the underlying body of all energy

Having said all this, I recommend that *The Book of the Five Rings* be read very attentively. It will be found to contain the application of the famous 'secret': the rule of the local and the global. When a man acts with the energy that is proper to him and at the time that is proper to him, he utilizes rhythms. Musashi notes that in every domain,—in music, the military arts, horse riding, archery—everything obeys a rhythm. Rhythm is like the underlying body of all energy. Time has its rhythms too, as does every human activity.

On the other hand, when a man acts with the energy of the global, which is one with the Whole or the Void itself, that man is Void. Of course we are not talking about nothingness. The Void is what contains and embraces the whole of reality. It is the body of all energies. It is the place where what is exists as if it were not. We would say today that what cannot be contained contains. And what contains governs and orders all content. The Void contains all things and is therefore the ultimate reality. 'Make the Void into the Way. And think of the Void as ''way'' [says Musashi] . . . for intelligence is ''being''. Ways are ''being''. But the mind is ''Void''.'

Naturally our rational minds may have a great deal of difficulty in grasping the nature of this way that Musashi is talking about. Therefore it is necessary to go back to the rules of tactics, one of which at least is perfectly comprehensible: 'What an expert does seems slow, but he never varies from the right rhythm.' When we apply this to the art of fighting, the result is as follows: 'If you try to cut too quickly with a sword, the sword does not cut at all.' Thus the first thing to do is to discover 'time' or the right rhythm of things. In our century of struggle with the watch, one might wonder whether man is not burning himself foolishly up in a vain struggle with time. The tragedy of modern days is that man, living outside the rhythm of the seasons, outside the rhythms of his own body, and outside the rhythms of his own psyche, is living ultimately outside himself. In this sense, the first rule of tactics would not be to struggle desperately for improved efficiency, nor to become a Machiavellian strategist, but to give natural laws their place again: then there is a strong likelihood that this inward living strategy will prove itself superior to any other strategy formulated according to the structures of the mind.

Man is in fact a 'warrior' in all his actions. But we must neither devalue nor excessively exalt this word. The magnates who have built up their business empires are indeed sometimes 'warriors' in their way, showing a combination of courage, intelligence, perspicacity, wisdom, and occasionally even an aptitude for meditation. Machiavelli was not a warrior. If a man lacks nobility of character, breadth of vision, precision in judgement, and above all the taste for battle (as opposed to confrontation), that man is no warrior. We have only to look around us, in the world in which we move, and we shall understand. The destiny of man goes beyond man. There is something in *The Book of the Five Rings* which transcends the treatise itself. If we could really understand that, we would be able to discover in it an endless number of fundamental keys and to become initiates ourselves through applying its principles. That is why I, too, want to say like Musashi: find out the effectiveness beyond effectiveness, beyond the forces of dynamization and ripening, become truly what you are, be decisive in applying the rules that operate in your own inner depths, practise the deep 'tactics' of your being. This is what will make you into a true warrior.

8. The soul of the sword

The sword is both weapon and symbol, and what it represents is highly significant. Its blade is so fine and hard as to make it almost immaterial. The flashing movement of the blade in a sword fight is almost instantaneous, almost as fast as the speed of a bullet from a revolver. The sword is sacred in Japanese thought. The forger who makes it imbues it with spiritual qualities, and to these are added the qualities of the swordsman. Thus, when a sword has been soaked in the blood of battle, when it has been in the hands of a courageous fighter, it becomes priceless. It becomes a complete symbol, an instrument redolent of the mystery of life and death.

All this heroic symbolism may seem alarming if the essentially spiritual element in it is not understood. Because it springs out instantaneously, the sword is the symbol of reality itself. Because it represents the absolute frontier of life and death, the sword demands absolute attention. The fighter who advances must be free in spirit and free in his heart. If he has not conquered fear, hatred and terror, he will inevitably succumb to the enemy's sword. The pure, serene fighter is just a metaphor, of course, but serenity has an unquestionable force. Nothing is fixed, everything is free and everything happens quickly: there is a way of fixing one's thought on the enemy in such a way as to see him pierced within one's own mind. Hence the saying that it is the victim himself who impales himself on the sword. What is impaled is in reality the fear, the terror or the hatred which inspires him. A restless spirit is invariably dominated by a calm one.

The Zen monk Takuan, who was born in 1573, understood the issue very clearly: he saw how all that is intention or idea is like a point or a fixation; every fixation makes a victim of itself. 'If you pay attention to the rhythm of the combat [he writes], your mind will be a prisoner of that rhythm. If you fix your attention on the sword, your mind will be the prisoner of the sword. The secret is to harmonize your sword with the sword of the enemy, to somehow manage to grasp it in its own field'.

The samurai continued to practise the art of weapons-handling throughout their lives. But only those with a true mastery of *ki* could go beyond mere force and virtuosity and make themselves invulnerable.

19. & 20. Terushige Shiokawa, master of the Shito-ryū karatē school, meditating and fighting. The school has a following estimated at 35,000. He is a accomplished master of all the martial arts.

The sword was the very soul of the samurai, it was precisely the weapon that transmitted *ki*. Before acquiring a sword, a true samurai would test it exhaustively. He would want to know who had forged it, where it was forged, the circumstances and the time of its fabrication. The choice of sword involved close analysis—of the hardness of its edge, the firmness and flexibility of its steel, the delicacy of the grain, the 'waves' engraved on the blade, and many other elements. But all this was still not enough. By definition a sword was lived, alive. To step over a sword was a great crime.

Indeed, a samurai rarely allowed himself to be separated from his

sword, except during the tea ceremony, when he had to leave it at
the entrance to the tea pavilion, or else when he was visiting friends,
and knew that the house was guarded. Then he would put his sword
on a sword-rack at the entrance. Before he took it off he would place
it on the ground and bow to it.

9. One arrow, one life

The reality of the target is actually beyond the target. When the target
is no longer separate from me, I can see the arrow hit the target before
it even leaves the bow. The visualization of what is is given to me
by the non-mental state that implies a state without knowledge, in
other words freed from the obstacle of techniques and from fixation
on the target. Eugen Herrigel explained this very well on the basis
of his own experience and his own efforts to learn to shoot. (But
remember this is not the type of shooting that is a popular sport in
the West.) The awareness we are talking about is not different in essence
from ordinary mental acuity. To apply the whole of one's energy to
the conquest of a point is to make manifest the whole reality of this
point, which grows into a kind of horizon for me. 'Free yourself from
yourself' said Awa, Herrigel's master, 'Abandon all that you are, tension
knows no purpose.'

Every particular intention is in itself an aim that alienates the
ultimate aim. I go innumerable ways to turn around one and the same
reality. What is asks only to reveal itself, to spring out like an arrow
or a sudden reality. The stability of things lies in being, wherever
that is. A tranquil mind can live in a noisy city. Although the right
external conditions are advantageous for serenity, true serenity actually
exists in itself. For the Japanese, a man is always facing his adversary.
When the blow springs out, when life itself is threatened,
imperturbable serenity is then known as *zanshin*.

The archer who aims does not shoot, for the target is not struck
when it is sought. Nevertheless, there is no sense in abandoning the
idea of aiming at the target. Yet is is horribly difficult to know a real
aim, the one that is bound up with one's destiny. People in general
are either overloaded with aims or they are simply aimless. Each one
shoots as he thinks opportune at the best moment. Long practice
in the technology of aims ought to teach us to anticipate all economic
surprises unerringly. But nothing could be further from the case. For

the real complexity is beyond our aims. We form a reality, and that takes on the forms which seem most propitious to us. But actual reality eludes us, veiled by its outward forms.

The master of reality is thus reality itself, or else the person who sees in the state of *mushin* (detachment from all things) what this reality really is, and withdraws from what is not actual reality: he thereby allows the forces of illusion to come into operation and proceed to the necessary explosion of illusory forms. The great somersaults of individual life and the history of societies amounts to nothing more than a trembling of reality that allows things to find their proper place. This awareness of the real is clearly visible in the practice of Japanese archery, *kyūdō*.

We owe our knowledge and appreciation of the great spiritual adventure of archery in particular to a German professor of philosophy named Herrigel. In 1932, Herrigel went to Tokyo to teach philosophy. He wanted to understand Zen. His old friend the jurist Komachya told him to go and see the master archer Awa (1880–1939). Awa agreed to teach Herrigel, after some hesitation on account of an earlier negative experience with a Westerner. Thus began an apprenticeship that was to last for five difficult years, at the end of which Herrigel had shown that a Westerner can succeed in understanding and practising *kyūdō*. He made a very favourable impression, and when he left Japan, he took with him as a present a bow belonging to Awa himself. Herrigel told the story of his apprenticeship and its happy conclusion in a marvellous little book: *Zen in the art of archery.**

And yet it was three years before Herrigel was finally allowed to use the bow to shoot at a target. Until then, a twofold teaching that was both spiritual and technical had taught him to bend the bow in reality and in the mind. To shoot, it is important that the mind should be serene, free and liberated from any thoughts about shooting. In practice, the difficulties that must be overcome to reach this state are innumerable. The aim is that the release of the arrow should be accomplished with accuracy and spontaneity. This imperative so obsessed Herrigel that he found a cunning method by which the shot seemed to be released spontaneously even while he was controlling it by the progressive slipping of his fingers bent back on his thumb.

His master Awa immediately grasped Herrigel's intention, made

* Most recent edition in English: London 1985.

him put the bow down, turned his back on him and sent him away. He had cheated, and the inevitable consequence was the definitive cessation of the teaching. It was only after many apologies and the intervention of his jurist friend that Herrigel's master Awa agreed to take up the lessons again.

One day, when Herrigel had just shot an arrow, the master bowed to the ground: 'Something has just shot an arrow' he cried. Indeed, a true shot had really happened. Thus the Great Doctrine had run its course and henceforth Herrigel knew how to 'dance the ceremony'; in other words, how to attain to that state of pure inner liberty in which the unity of perfectly harmonized being—body, mind, arrow and breathing—made it possible to sense what constitutes a perfect shot: that moment at which a man has become without thought so that the arrow of being can be shot. This is why the old saying goes 'One arrow, one life.' We shoot our whole life in every arrow. Thus we must aim further than the target and beyond the apparent target. After the arrow has left the bow, the archer stays for a moment in an attitude of concentration and meditation called *zanshin*. This means that in his mind he is following the shooting of the arrow.

In spite of all his progress, Herrigel only rarely managed to hit a target at 60 metres. He consulted his teacher anxiously about this, and the gist of the latter's reply was that the goal was not simply a matter of striking the target, for even were he to attain a 100 percent strike rate, that would merely put him on the level of a circus performer. The Great Doctrine views it as diabolical to make an idol out of success. The desired goal cannot be reached by the use of purely technical means. Otherwise the target would be nothing but a useless bit of paper, and the goal would not be the Buddha. Target-shooting without a target rests on the awakening of a rhythm and a harmony that are internal to things and beings. The archer hits his target, but outwardly he does not aim at it. 'In that case', observed Herrigel, 'you ought to be able to hit a target blindfold'. 'Come round this evening', was the teacher's reply.

That evening, Awa asked Herrigel to place something in front of the target. It was a tall mosquito candle, as thin as a knitting-needle. The target was almost invisible: there was only the miniscule gleam of the mosquito candle to illuminate it.

'The first arrow', writes Herrigel, 'whipped out of the glare and sped away into the black night. I could tell by the sound made on impact

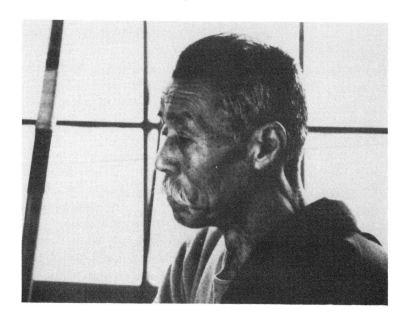

21. Anzawa the master, at 82.

that it had hit the target. The second struck home too. I put on the lights of the shooting gallery and discovered to my utter amazement that the first arrow was in the bull's eye, while the second had shattered the nock of the first, split its stem in two, and finally buried itself in the bullseye as well.'

'Something was shooting and something hit the target', observed the master. Although I myself did not know Awa, I did know the grand master Anzawa who succeeded him and who was in his younger day's Awa's pupil at the same time as Herrigel. Our first meeting took place in 1968 at Anzawa's house in the Tokyo suburbs. I was there with a team from French television. And for the first time in his life he agreed to be filmed, at the age of 81. This brief documentary, just a few minutes long, is all that remains as a record of him.

Seated in the lotus position, Anzawa, the greatest grand master of the bow in Japan (he died in 1970), was meditating. The noise of the city could be heard in the *dōjō*—the training gallery he had installed at the bottom of his garden—but he heard nothing: he was creating silence within himself. Then, moving his body with incredible

22. Anzawa shooting. 'One arrow, one life.' Man, bow, arrow and target have become one.

deliberateness, he knelt down with his bow at his left side, until he was touching the ground. His feet were clad in white slippers held on by the big toes, and they slid gently along the brightly-polished floor. It was as if we were present at a choreographed performance by some *nō* theatre group, in which the smallest gesture was made to last for an eternity. Finally he got up, executed several movements, glided forward, bared his left shoulder, knelt down again and remained still. Then he seized the bow, lined up a white-feathered arrow and took up a second arrow which he gripped with his fingers while he positioned the first to shoot. The axis of the bow slowly rose to head-height and the bow was turned towards the target: suddenly, as if the long-drawn out tension had reached an unbearable climax, the arrow flew off to the sound of a short, sharp and powerful cry—the *kiai*.

For a brief moment the master's look lingered on the target, while the arrow carried on in his spirit: it was the very symbol of energy, and nothing could stop it. 'One arrow, one life', Anzawa used to say. Then he gradually emerged from his reverie, his concentration relaxed, and the arrow ceased to have importance for him, as the master came back to himself. If he was not planning to shoot a second arrow, he would glide to the back of the *dōjō*, put the bow down, and bend his body reverently before it until his forehead was touching the floor. He had lived a perfect shot.

The whole exercise had taken at least half an hour, from the moment when he had picked up his bow to the moment when he had shot his first arrow. For the duration of this half-hour, the master had isolated himself from everything but the thought of the shot; his inner concentration had worked the alchemy of unity; the man, the bow, the arrow and the target had become one. Success at bowmanship and the spiritual function of the art reside in the acquisition of this perfect unity. It is the point of concentration which will release the arrow with innocence and forgetfulness: perfect non-willing is what will perform the shot, and thereby attain the true goal.

10. The way of the bow and the horse

The way of the bow and the horse was the first samurai code at the end of the twelfth century. But despite the similarity in meaning it is much more appropriate to speak of a *way* than of a code. Traditionally, a way is that which engages the totality of a man as a whole being.

A code is a juridical entity which is to be obeyed, whether voluntarily or under constraint. Furthermore, a way offers the idea of a process of perfecting oneself that is continuous and indeed unlimited. It was not until much later that 'code' and 'way' were defined by one single word: *Bushidō*, which means 'the way of the warrior or the knight.' According to Pierre Land, Bushido comes from 'a long heritage of precepts—Shinto, Buddhist, Confucian, National, Chinese or derived from the strict customs of a rural people. It embraces veneration for ancestors, obedience to the sovereign, uprightness of mind and heart, patience, resignation to the inevitable and contempt for death. In spite of all these other influences, Bushidō remains an expression of the peculiarly hard and pure Japanese character.

Down through the centuries, numerous books have expounded in great detail the qualities requisite for the way of the warrior. The best known are the *Budō Shoshin* or *Elementary Lectures on Bushidō*, written by an erudite samurai, Daidoji Yuzan (1639–1730), and the *Kōyō Gunkan* (early seventeenth century), running to about 20 volumes and attributed to Kosaka Danjo Masanobu. Either this is a *nom-de-plume* for Obata Kagenori (1572–1662) or else he was Kagenori's collaborator. The work sets up as a model Takeda Shingen, a great samurai and lord of the province of Suruga, a warrior who was never defeated. 'Every contest we enter we must win' is the fundamental idea of the *Gunkan*.

The way of the bow and the horse (Kyūba no Michi) is derived in part from the teachings of Chinese authorities on Archery, involving the use of different sorts of bows: the war bow, the hunting bow, archery on foot, archery on horseback, etc. But it was in the era of the Taira and Minamoto clans in the second half of the twelfth century that *The way of the bow and the horse* found its true significance. The bow became the weapon par excellence, to such an extent that the warrior was known as 'the one who carries the bow and arrow'. For centuries, however, the warrior's bow had been considered as much more than a weapon, it had been seen as the symbol of that being to which the warrior must assimilate himself, thereby proving the degree of his spiritual elevation. The bow and arrow were an essential combat weapon and did not lose their supremacy over all others until the emergence of the arquebus in the middle of the sixteenth century. Today it is difficult for us to conceive the level of perfection and refinement attained at that time in the technique of the bow and arrow.

The purely warrior-like aspects of *kyūjutsu* soon became ennobled under the form of *kyūdo*.

The cult of the bow
Paradoxically, we owe the characteristic shape of the famous Japanese bow to the invasion of Japan by the Mongols in the thirteenth century. It was actually in the course of this invasion that the Japanese discovered the Mongol bows, built up from a somewhat thin 'soul' of supple wood and armoured with pieces of horn on the inner side as well as on the back. On top of this there were two or three levels of bovine tendon, and the whole was stuck together and placed in a mould to force the bow into its definitive shape. The Japanese succeeded in adapting this mode of manufacture and utilized bamboo as the foundational material, reinforcing it with different woods: mulberry and cherry (wild or domestic). The strips were glued together and put through rattan rings or woven round with bamboo bark. Japanese bows thus eventually took on the definitive form that they were to retain up till modern times.

23. Detail of a posture of Master Onuma. The target is a distant mirror that summons the arrow.

Of all the impressive variety of bows of every size and dimension that have been seen down the years, Japanese warriors settled on one that was particularly tricky to handle and not overly practical; a long bow running to 2.20 or up to 2.40 metres long (and sometimes even longer) with the sinuous form of a double curve. The grip from which this bow is stretched is 73 centimetres from the bottom of the bow, so that tension is exercised more or less over one-third of the length of the bow. This exceptional length has remained peculiar to the Japanese bows. All the other peoples in the East—the Chinese, the Koreans and the Mongols—adopted shorter bows (1.20 metres) that were easier to carry. They are normally stretched from the middle of the curve, and the Japanese is the only bow to be held below the middle of the curve.

The Japanese have always regarded the bow with a veneration far greater than what is merited by its military use. To find any equivalent cult of the bow we have to go as far back as the Assyrians. The Assyrian bow was precisely one of the few types in the ancient world to be like the Japanese. And just as for the Assyrians the bow and arrow were sacred objects when they belonged to kings or generals, likewise for the Japanese the supreme way is the way of the sword and the bow. To master the weapon perfectly means to harmonize the pressures which make it so difficult to use, and to synchronize the tension of the bow, which tends to turn in the hands, with that of the string: it also requires the skilful placing of the long arrow, with its tendency to swerve off upwards. These manoeuvres require long practice, perfect body balance, and profound concentration.

The champions of Sanjūsangendō

The greatest Japanese bowmen have always competed at the Buddhist temple of *Sanjūsangendō* at Kyōto. There the archer takes up a north-facing posture; the target is 1.74 metres across and stands about 18 metres away. The difficulty for the shooter resides in the fact that he is hemmed in to the right by the angle of the roof and, more to the point, he is limited by the lowness of the roof, which is only 3.80 metres from the floor. At such a distance, the arrow that follows a slightly curving trajectory tends to strike a big beam supporting the roof. It is therefore crucial to choose a powerful bow that makes a straight shot possible but which is not so hard to draw that it restricts the number of shots: for the aim of the competition is to put as many arrows as possible into the target in the course of one day.

Shooting begins at dawn. The greatest exploit ever known in this contest was accomplished in 1686 and has never been repeated. The names of the shooters were Wasa Daiachirō and Hoshino Kanzaemon. After he had shot 7,850 arrows (a rate of about 9 a minute), Wasa found his shoulders were swollen with blood and his rate was slowing. Despite his talent and courage, he was in danger of being beaten by Hoshino, who had hit the target 8,000 times. Hoshino saw that his rival was in difficulty and was quick to help him. At a stroke he cut an incision with his little sword (*shotō*) in the most swollen part of Wasa's shoulders. The blood flowed, and the relieved bowman managed to place 8,133 arrows, which made him the winner of the contest. It is calculated that if we take into account the failed arrows, Wasa shot 13,053 arrows during that day. As for Hoshino, he carried off the palm of honour. The story enables us to understand better the Japanese expression 'house of bows and arrows' to indicate a person's nobility of character.

In Shinto, the arrow is often an aid to purification. Various temples sell arrows intended to carry away all the impurities and ill omens that accumulate in a house as the year progresses. These arrows are then burned in the end-of-year ceremonies.

Numbering infinity

The arrows are made according to a set of rules which ensure that manual work is never separated from spiritual. The arrows are cut at the time of the winter solstice, then they are left to dry for two or three months. The bamboo used has to be perfectly suited, and only one bamboo out of 200 will be just right. The bamboo chosen has to be very straight, and although all bamboos have knots, these must not be too prominent. Three-year old bamboos are therefore generally preferred: younger than this they are usually too soft, and later on they become too hard. Furthermore, the arrows must not be either too light or too heavy. If the bow is firm, the arrows must be solid and hard. If the bow is a light one, the arrows must of course be matched accordingly. The trickiest part is finding arrows of a uniform quality.

There used to be arrows that had a sort of ball on the end which would produce blood-curdling noises as they sped through the air. Even the length of the arrow is fortunate or baleful: if it is 2 feet

8 inches (79cm) it is held to be lucky. In Shinto tradition, in fact, the sign '8' means 'circle'. It is the figure for infinity; in other words, for the indeterminate number of things: 8, 88, 888, 8888, etc.

The feathers on the arrows also have a meaning. If white feathers are chosen, it is because they chase away the wicked spirits which hide in dark places. The arrow with white eagle's feathers is always the first one to be fired. It serves not simply to pinpoint the target temporarily but also to ward off evil spells. The other four bamboo arrows are a little shorter and are lined with fine grooves: they are split into twos and must be shot in a certain fixed order.

The archer pierces the heavens
In archery conducted with the traditional ceremonies, the five arrows are put into a quiver made out of cherry wood. The Japanese know that only the bamboo arrow gives them the sensory pleasure provided by the clarity of the sound made by the string as the arrow leaves the bow. Their bow has another peculiar feature: it is made in such a way that it is twice as light above the grip as it is below. When it is drawn, its asymmetrical length gives the shooting movement a kind of beauty, while also allowing for a significant spreading out of the effort between the two arms equally.

The practice of bowmanship thus remains essentially an exercise in serenity and spiritual discipline. 'True art', Anzawa used to say, 'has no goal or intention. The more one strives to attain an objective, the less one succeeds. The obstacle is the excessive concentration of the will on an aim. We also say: With one end of the bow, the archer pierces the heavens: at the other end there is a silken link to the earth. if the archer shoots in too violent a fashion, the risk is that the link may break. Then a man is left between heaven and earth in an intermediate position that offers no salvation.'

This inner attitude is defined by the expression: 'Do not hold your mind in any particular place'. This maxim is the one that Takuan repeats in all kinds of different ways in his collection *Mysteries of motionless wisdom*. Motionlessness here means 'non-fixation'. In modern physics we speak of a kind of non-localization. Because properties are what they are, these properties remain constants and corollaries, and so instantaneous and synchronized, whatever the distance in space or time. Not fixing one's mind means using the spontaneity of time differently. As soon as I have understood this, it is the dance that lifts my arm, a movement that is as sudden and rapid as a seemingly contained and motionless dance, and yet none the less with its profound presence and by a kind of double attention it keeps all the molecules of my body and all the neurones of my thought in movement. The apparent immobility masks the dynamism of consciousness. The motionless wisdom of the Buddha is the contrary of a static reality. The centre of motionless wisdom resembles the centre of all centres. It is potentiality. It is the positive-negative action of the *yin-yang*, it is those coiled-up forces that are like the reality of a particle at once vectorial and vibratory, it is one single reality.

Reality is omnipresent. It is not in the mind, nor in the body, nor in the Universe. It is in the mind-body-Universe, and all at the same time too. This unity-spontaneity is difficult for a Westerner to grasp. The only things we understand are those which are separated, divided, fragmented, and offered as formulae with a simple application. But simplicity itself, that simplicity which calls for us not to be fixed on any single point, but to allow all points to be homogeneous and constant among themselves, this simplicity seems incomprehensible to us and totally inapplicable to daily life. And yet it is a permanent hidden constant of the Japanese mind.

11. *The science of energy and the spirit of ki*

The concept of *ki*, (or *chi* in Chinese), is like that of *hara* in Japan, the equivalent of the Chinese 'field of cinnabar'. The nuance in interpretation and sensation, if I may call it that, is in both cases significant in terms of what distinguishes two cultures that are nonetheless still very close to each other.

The traditional Chinese philosophy of Tao or Dao is all-embracing. The Tao expresses the source of all things, from which all things come and to which they all return; it is not a reality, and it is not a non-reality either. The Tao derives from an infinitesimal substance or energy, and that energy is *ki*.

The Japanese *ki* is more focused. It embraces all things, but at the same time it pierces everything. It both binds and splits. The energy of *ki* becomes a strategy when the intention is mastery over self or over the other. Without *ki*, there can be no Japanese martial arts. Likewise, in the thick of the economic battle, every leader or business chief in Japan will never cease to manifest the same stubborn, perceptive, and persevering *ki* as his colleagues.

One of the surprises of the Tsukuba colloquium in November 1984 was that every one of the Japanese participants expounded the philosophy of *ki*, though each did it differently. To the astonished Western scientists, the Japanese philosophers and scientists seemed to be talking a different language. This is clear proof that *ki* is a concept to which the Japanese still accord the highest possible importance. We must therefore try to understand what this *ki* really means.

The basis of all oriental thought is this: the world understood as an expression of universal harmony, the universe understood as a total integration of man into the harmony of which he is the perfect expression. On this foundation is built a conception of the body and of underlying energies and their interactions. An understanding of this underlying physiology makes it possible to deduce a whole series of applications in bodily discipline, in mental hygiene, in medicine, and in art.

As soon as we leave the level of measurable and quantifiable energies, we have to imagine energies of an increasingly subtle nature, and thought as a part of these. Hence what we might call an 'energy of interactions', which are nothing more than a sort of potentialization of our fields of awareness. Ultimately, the nature of the real always depends on the awareness or vision we have of it. This leads us into ever sharper states of perception. Thus we are led to conceive a sort of analogy that is both real and symbolic between what might look like a 'number for man' resulting from the constant harmonious laws of the Universe, and his own physiology. Whence comes the concept of meridians, which in Chinese and Japanese tradition are invisible circuits through which this energy is manifested, and the concept of the *chakra*, in Hindu tradition, which correspond ultimately to the development both of this same energy and of the knowledge of the various states of being aroused by this energy.

When we consider all things on the first level of reality, we can analyze them according to their physical or chemical properties, which are constant. But these properties change as soon as thought intervenes. Energy-thought or energy-consciousness develops a vibratory field which operates in the manner of an alchemical process, in the sense that it 'crystallizes' or brings about the appearance of properties that belong to this vibratory field. Thus there is a modification of states, perceptions and energies, and also a modification of physical, chemical, and physiological properties on the first level. Hence the air we breathe reveals its igneous principle, its energy that is assimilable to fire, *prana*. Likewise, breathing the oxygen of the air is a quite spontaneous action. But if we add to this breathing a particular attention of the mind, our thought potentializes the molecules of the air in the most intense fashion and gives them a different quality. That is the art of breathing.

Christian tradition too, has a similar conception, that of *pneuma* which also means breath. Breath engenders an energy which can absorb all sorts of qualities. It is open to each tradition and discipline to express through their own particular sensibility and their experiential or sensorial knowledge this new concept of an energy activated by the consciousness-field or by thought. The Polynesians use the word *mana*; the science of yoga is associated with a physiology of states of being and to an understanding of the energy that binds together these states, namely *kundalini*. This is a vital energy, a serpent of fire which can descend or climb, become spiritualized or manifest the mystery of chaos. China, tied to a more imponderable conception, that of Tao, will thus conceive this concept of energy as all-embracing. It is *chi*. Japan has a natural tendency to potentialize this energy and give it a more precise, more vectorial function as it were. It is *ki*, and it can be known at once in its cosmological manifestation and also in precisely directed applications. Whence the application of *ki* in the martial arts.

Ki is both universal and physiological, it is both an ontological and a scientific mode of comprehension: this gives rise to ambiguity. A further ambiguity surrounds the fields in which *ki* is actually applied and where the two aspects mentioned above manifest themselves, whether simultaneously or separately. What is really needed, then, is a rigorous study that would make an inventory of these different states of *ki*. But here Western thought finds itself completely wrong-footed. For neither the epistemological nor the scientific attitude is ultimately capable of coming to grips with a phenomenon that is assimilable to a sort of spontaneous fusion. We therefore have to be extremely cautious in our attempts to prove that a particular state is identifiable with the aid of encephalograms or of measures designed to determine physiological changes. At the most such measures reveal that something is happening, without there being any real possibility of defining what exactly it is. Moreover, every observation modifies the actual nature of what is observed: there is an interaction between observer and observed.

The observable effects of ki

It is nonetheless true that the Earth turns and that the reality of subtle energies potentialized by thought and by the consciousness-field is a true reality. A more rational type of research involves observing the effects of *ki*—if we restrict ourselves to this one example for the time being—in adepts, and situating their particular experience in the context of a tradition that is both well established and explicit. The interaction of energy-thought may take on innumerable forms; it varies according to the individual and according to the different states of the individual. Analysis cannot grasp infinitely variable energies, but it can observe their effects. There is a technique for the acquisition and development of *ki*, an art of breathing, and another technique for correctly gathering energies into the *hara* (or central point situated two centimetres below the navel according to Japanese tradition). But one can no more draw up an inventory of *ki* than of the unity of the Universe itself. *Ki* exists. That stated, it becomes what we make of it. It can be positive or negative, liberating or destructive. It is nothing but a very concrete and also very abstract manifestation of the universal energy received and modified by man. The science of *ki* exists in the sense that it is experimental in the individual himself. It is a particular state of the energies and the mind at a given moment. This state can be stabilized, whence the science of its practice, or on the other hand it may be constantly variable. The effects of *ki* are visible, but *ki* itself remains for ever invisible.

These brief observations have no other aim than to indicate the existence of an exciting field for research and application. But the apprehension of this field requires the utmost clarity of observation, and it must be remembered that the complexity of the interactions resulting from the practice of *ki* has an essentially physiological character, even though this underlying physiology remains in itself beyond the scope of analysis.

12. Ki and aikidō: the teaching of the master Morihei Ueshiba

Basically *aikidō* signifies the way (*dō*) of union or love (*ai*) with the breath or spirit (*ki*). This art is very close to archery by its metaphysical content. It illustrates the fundamental idea that the body can be totally controlled by the mind. The important thing is that body and mind remain in unison with nature and that movement should be like a breath. Then each gesture is a way of pouring oneself into a movement

24. Master Morihei Ueshiba, with Michio Hikitsuchi (Tenth dan), who was to be his greatest disciple, at his side. Even in Japan there are few who understand the uniqueness of Ueshiba. The outward part of his teaching conceals a human and spiritual depth that is still mysterious.

that resembles breathing or music.

In *aikidō* the secret is to make a void, directing it either against the adversary, who thus finds himself as it were enclosed in a circle from which he cannot escape, or drawing him into the void of one's own circle. 'When an enemy tries to fight me, he is fighting the Universe itself, and he has to break the harmony of the Universe', said Ueshiba Morihei, founder of modern *aikidō*. 'Thus, the moment he forms the intention to fight with me, he is already beaten. *Aikidō* is non-resistance: since it is non-resistance, it is always victorious.'

Ueshiba Morihei was undoubtedly a master at achieving the perfect union of energies or *ki*. He gave brilliant demonstrations of this power every day, proving how inner force can easily master brute force. This was not however sufficient to convince one powerful adept of karate. 'I don't care what you say', he said to him, 'I weigh 80 kilos, and if I hit you you will fly six metres off the ground.' Morihei himself hardly weighed more than 57 kilos. 'Not a bit of it', said he, his face wreathed in smiles. The karate expert was so insistent that a duel was planned. It was to be held in public. On the day, after all the customary ceremonial, Ueshiba positioned himself with bare chest in front of his opponent. The latter ran up and struck him a violent blow on the chest. He might just as well have hit the air, for the master stood looking calmly at him, not blinking an eyelid. 'Try again, please,' he said to the very disconcerted young man.

The young man ran up again and hit out with all his strength. This time the master remained as motionless as the first time, but the karate expert shrieked with pain. His wrist had been broken. The lesson was taken. The first time, in fact, the master had contented himself with absorbing the blow, he had met it with non-resistance. The second time, however, he had produced a rebound of his adversary's energy, and the latter had somehow received back the force of his own blow, only ten times stronger, with the result that his wrist had been broken.

Stories of this kind are very numerous in the life of Ueshiba Morihei. He could never be caught out or made vulnerable. Whatever the skill and rapidity of his adversary, the man was invariably sent flying, even when the master seemed to be relaxed: the angle of attack made no difference. One day, at the time of the Mongolian War, the master saw a Chinese soldier aiming a pistol at him. The man was about six metres away, but he disarmed him in a flash before anyone knew what was happening. 'How did you do it?' they asked him. 'There's a very long interval', answered Ueshiba Morihei, 'between the moment when a man forms his intention to kill you and the moment when he actually pulls the trigger.' This 'very long interval', the merest fraction of a second no doubt, had been enough for him to disarm his enemy.

In other words, the development of *ki* gives a person a different sense of time. As a rule, a practitioner of the martial arts becomes aware of this phenomenon quite quickly. Time no longer has the same duration. The gestures of opponents are instantaneously perceived as if in slow motion. Time has speeded up to an incredible extent.

Ueshiba's astonishing exploits would fill several volumes. Not only were they actually witnessed by many of our contemporaries, but they were in many cases actually filmed or photographed.

One day he was unwell and one of his disciples wanted to lift him up to put him to bed. The task was too difficult so he asked another young fellow to help him: they in turn had to enlist the help of a third and then a fourth. They all struggled vainly to lift the master.

He seemed glued to the ground. Eventually he seemed to wake up as if he had been asleep. 'I'm sorry', he said, 'I had bound heaven to earth within myself.' He seemed to relax, and all of a sudden be became as light as a feather and they were able to lift him. Such stories are familiar to all martial arts teachers. 'I can tell whether a man has *ki* or not simply by looking at the way he walks', one master used to say.

Ever since childhood, Ueshiba Morihei had had a weak constitution and poor health. But he had an iron will. So at the age of 14 he sought out the old masters of *jūjutsu*, and they taught him their art. At the age of 28 he took up with the master of masters—an astonishing man, Takeda Sōkaku, who had withdrawn to northern Japan to the remote Hokkaido area. Master Takeda was very short, exceptionally strong, and exceedingly severe. He set great store by the fact that he belonged to an ancient line, a branch of the famous Minamoto family. As for his particular kind of teaching, he attributed it, in accordance with venerable tradition, to Prince Sadazumi (874–916), the sixth son of the emperor Seiwa, said to have been the creator of the earliest forms of *aikijitsu* through the Daito school. This secret teaching was said to have been transmitted to Minamoto Yoshimitsu. The latter lived at Takeda in the province of Kai, and had taken the name of his locality; subsequently the secret principles of *aikijitsu* were handed down form generation to generation within the Takeda family.

In 1868, which was during the Meiji period, Takeda Sōkaku, the head of the family, opened a private school, the *Daitō School* in the Hokkaidō region. This was the first time that pupils from outside the family were taken in by the master. However, only persons of distinction, such as members of the Imperial family, together with a few other exceptional cases, were privileged to benefit from such teaching.

Thus Takeda Sōkaku was a master who was supremely sure of his own importance and the value of what he had to teach. In Ueshiba Morihei he recognized someone who at the age of 28 was already gifted with exceptional skill and who possessed an impressive degree of self-mastery. He praised Morihei for these accomplishments and took him on as a pupil. However, he did not make life easy for the young disciple. Ueshiba Morihei had to submit uncomplainingly to the master's extreme authoritarianism, he had to consecrate himself to the master, body and soul, serving him when called on at any hour of the day or night, preparing his meals and his baths, and even building him a new home. Furthermore, he had to pay the master between 300 and 500 yen for the teaching of each new technique, and at the time this was a considerable sum. And yet the days of actual teaching were few and far between. Over a five-year period the master devoted about 100 days to him. The rest of the time the pupil had to train on his own. It was not until 1916, when he was 33, that Ueshiba Morihei received the first diploma that named him a master of *jūjutsu* as practised by the Daito school. It is from this teaching that the substance of modern aikido is derived.

13. *The way of the sword and kendō*

Kendō or the way of the sword was the supreme art of the samurai. Japanese swordsmanship is very different from the western variety, for it is primarily offensive, while in the West the emphasis is above all on parrying blows and on progressively disabling the opponent until he can eventually be finished off. In *kendō* the first stroke must in practice be decisive. It therefore requires great courage; the samurai stood facing each other, holding their long swords in their hands, and it was not infrequent for one of the fighters to be cut in two.

Kendō is practised with a kind of long stick, the *shinai*, made out of four polished bamboo blades held together by leather thongs. The hands are protected by a thick round leather guard, the body by armour and the head by a helmet.

It is hard to practise this skill without knowing the spirit of *Bushido*. The *shinai* bears the spirit of the sword, which was, as we have said, in some sense the soul of the samurai. It represented all the potentialities of life and death. Only an inspired artist could forge a sword. He would begin his work by praying, 'binding his soul and spirit to the steel he was forging'.

Still today old swords are the object of devout veneration. This state of mind implies an extreme awareness in the act of drawing the sword. Any samurai who performed the action thoughtlessly would have been dishonoured.

From the age of three or four, boys and girls can learn *kendō*, says master Takano, from Kamakura. 'The practice of *kendō* allows children to develop all sorts of qualities. Children love to hit each other with any implement they can get hold of. *Kendō* channels these impulses. It becomes very pleasant for the child to put his energy into wielding the *shinai* while knowing that with armour and helmet on he won't end up being hurt.'

Takano of Kamakura was a very great master of *kendō*. Among his pupils were numbered the famous *kendō* team belonging to the Imperial guard. He had numerous little pupils, and the children loved to be taught by this master who could be so severe and yet so good-natured; he seemed much more like a grandfather than a great *kendō* master. But in the *dōjo* Takano was very much the master. It was extraordinary to see these children of not more than six or seven sitting in a perfect lotus position and beginning every session with a ten-minute meditation.

25. The oldest of these young kendōka is not yet six. They are pupils of Master Takano at Kamakura. The apprenticeship of the future samurais of industry begins when they are very young.

After meditating the children would greet the master and recite together the following precepts:

> We love our country
> We respect our parents
> We respect the ceremonies of our
>   traditions
> We respect our teaching
> We will do our duty

> We respect our comrades
> We swear to make ourselves healthy
>   in mind and body

Now the training could begin in earnest. The dōjō was near the beach. Training was conducted there, because it was a long way from the noise of the town. The master's presence was totally unobtrusive, since the children had grown accustomed to disciplining themselves. As soon as they got to the beach, they would gather soberly into one long line. They would place their equipment in front of them. then, when the master gave the word, they would put it on. The basic instruction includes the correct method of putting on the protective equipment—the helmet (*men*), the breastplate (*dō*), the gloves (*kote*), and the covering for the abdomen (*tare*).

Once the children were ready, training would begin. They demonstrated their skills in twos in front of the master. They performed exercises involving attacks aimed at the forehead (*men*), the mid-forehead (*sho men*), the right side of the forehead (*migi men*), the left side of the forehead (*hidari men*), the forearm (*kote*), etc. With every blow they practised shouting the name of the blow. They could be heard to shout '*Men*', '*Kote*', or '*Tare*'. These are the three basic attacking points, forehead, forearm, and flank. The children were not actually allowed to go for the opponent's throat (i.e. to do *tsuki*) until they were 16 years old.

After this series of mini-sessions, the children let off steam in a communal fight. They set to with howls of delight and pleasure. The *shinai* banged together and the blows rained down in rapid succession. It was great fun to watch all these little *kendōka* having such a wonderful time and showing such delight on the beach. All grand masters of *kendō* spend a part of their time teaching very young children. This is a task they undertake with a special affection and interest, as they are exhorted to do by the rule of *kendō* itself. It is never too early to have one's mind and body moulded and to be given a vigorous soul.

Once the training session was over, the children would form up into a line again. Then they very calmly returned to the *dōjō*, where they took off their equipment. The session would end with a final short meditation and a greeting to the master. In short, everyone had a marvellous time.

1. The kiai

In children, *Kendō* develops the habit of mobilizing the mental and physical energies completely in a very short space of time. Naturally the children do not show particular swiftness in their actions. What they shout are not the *kiai*, but just shrill cries.

At the moment of attack, adversaries utter a cry: the *kiai*. This cry is particularly impressive in *kendō*. Each school has its own type of *kiai*. Certain Western novelists have spoken of the *kiai* as the cry that kills. It does not of course kill by itself: its purpose is to distract the adversary at the very moment he is being attacked. The pupil learns to utter the *kiai* in such a way that it comes straight from the stomach, in other words, directly from the true centre of energy. A cry uttered suddenly from the back of the throat is completely ineffective. The learner soon finds out how to discern the place the cry is coming from, he is soon able to sense whether it is laden with psychic energy or whether it is merely a guttural noise. Of a pair of adversaries it is the one with the strongest *kiai* who will in practise overcome the other. The sudden vibration of the *kiai* imposes its superiority instantaneously. *Kiai* contains *ki*. The person who has the greatest mastery of *ki* (cosmic energy) will of necessity dominate others. The power of *kiai* acts in the mental and psychic realms both at once. It is an impersonal cosmic energy that strikes at the psychic and personal part of the opponent. The Universe against the self. But there are also *kiai* that come from within and they are silent. The person who has mastered such a secret *kiai* can strike his adversary without the latter knowing it. Thus the victim is struck by this 'energy-thought' at a moment of weakness. Such a *kiai* can be acquired through the practice of inner respiration (breath) directed by thought, and in conjunction with exercises of the *hara* (stomach or centre).

All the martial arts teachers emphasize the fact that a man can do nothing until he knows how to concentrate and liberate the energy of the *hara*, or stomach. To that end there are, in karate for example, special respiration techniques called *ibuki*. Such respiration can also be practised in a spectacular manner, underneath a waterfall. The shock of the water falling of to the top of the skull has the effect of encouraging a particular state of concentration.

Energy is the stronger insofar as it is liberated at one and the same point. The possession of such a concentration and respiration is called *kokyū*. When two masters are equals from the point of view of technique, you can be certain that the victor will be the one whose *kokyū* is the stronger. It is difficult to explain the effect of *kokyū*; it finds expression in the power somehow to direct the whole of one's psychic and physical energy onto one single point. This makes a man mysteriously invulnerable.

The idea of concentrating the totality of one's energy on one point is the basis of all the martial arts. Without energy a blow has no power. The smaller the surface struck, the more powerful the blow. If, on top of this, there is a very precise knowledge of the most vulnerable points in the body, it is obvious what lethal precision can be inculcated by such a science.

2. Serenity and self-mastery
With older children, it is possible to discern a difference between those who have practised kendō from infancy and those who have taken up the practice of it relatively late. The difference must have something to do with the greater spontaneity of the blows and the manifestly more developed powers of intuition. The objective of kendō is to institute an attack-defence tactic of extreme rapidity, such that every attack can be transformed instantaneously into defence and inversely. The ultimate rule is to strike the decisive fatal blow.

If the blow is to spring out like lightning, the *kendōka* must devote himself to a very extensive course of training. It will take him years and years before he learns to project his energy onto the point of the *shinai*. Only a minority of the children will manage to make a blow spring out as fast as a revolver bullet. This ultimate secret is that of the great masters: it is the art of delivering blows so lightly that the *shinai* seems only to graze the adversary, and yet he is hurled senseless.

'The important thing', says Takano, 'is to learn serenity and self-mastery from the moment you are out of your nappies. Children must learn to visualize the blow with their inner vision. If the movement is first of all lived through in the mind, then it can spring out more easily at the moment of delivery.'

The practitioner is driven to the limit of his potential. That is why all such training is so lengthy. The samurai of old used to train from their earliest years with short or long sticks. Still today this teaching is carried on in the school of *Araki-ryū*. This is the only school in Japan where the tradition of white sticks still persists. These sticks foreshadowed kendō, and made it possible to train protected only by gloves and something over the head and the ears. Of course, there were frequent accidents. Still, the young folk I saw training in the *Araki-Ryū* school seemed very skilful at delivering and avoiding blows without injuring themselves in the slightest.

3. The education of the look

Master Takano accorded a particular importance to the look. He used to say that one must always look at the adversary as one would look at a distant mountain. The important thing is thus to see and at the same time not to see the adversary so as to sense the blow that is about to spring out. That is why it is said that the eye represents the mind. The trick is to penetrate the eyes of the enemy so as to sense what he is thinking: and not simply to observe him in his eyes, but also to guess him in his overall movement. In other words, it is necessary to learn to see the point of the *shinai* and the movement of the hands with one and the same look. Kendō is the look that goes further than a look.

The deeper meaning here is that the energies must be concentrated effectively on this global vision. In other words, 'seeing through one's mind' means seeing right through the adversary even while remaining outwardly gentle and calm.

This question of the look plays a considerable part in kendō. As a rule, the practitioner imagines that if he shows sufficient ardour he will be able to improve his techniques for coping with attacks. Of course it is important to know how to move rapidly on one's feet and to make blows spring out with lightning speed. But all this is still subordinate to observation of the adversary. Such observation must be spontaneous. It is necessary to sum up who the opponent is and what his psychological and psychic structure is. A kendōka armed from head to foot looks alarmingly intimidating. And yet I have seen adults beaten by young kendōka of 14 or 15 years old, probably because these youths possessed a sensitivity that enabled them to guess their adversary and so to dominate him more intuitively, in spite of their tender years and lesser experience.

4. The three rules of attack

There are three fundamental rules in kendō. One consists in attacking the opponent's *shinai*, the second in attacking his technique (*waza*) and the third in attacking his mind.

The first of these three attacks involves controlling the point of the *shinai*. Each kendōka actually sets out to control the centre of his opponent with the point of his own *shinai*. Thus there ensues a battle for the control of this centre. The riposte is of course to attack the *shinai* in such a way that it cannot master your centre. The second method consists in discovering the opponent's favourite technique and then utilizing it to one's own advantage. The third rule consists in attacking your opponent's mind, by uttering louder and more piercing shrieks than him.

26. In kendō the rule is lightning attack. The shouts—the kiai—are often terrifying. Here Takano is watching. The fundamental rule is still powerful: attack the opponent's mind, and your skill will do the rest.

Of course, there are a huge variety of attacks and defences, and these can be appreciated fully only through practice.

Fear must be mastered. The practitioner is driven to the limit of his potential. The struggle is violent and swift. It is when one is mentally and physically exhausted that one learns to deliver blows correctly. Another force comes to replace brute mental and physical force. This state is called *kirikaeshi* and according to a Japanese proverb, it gives 'ten powers to the attacker and eight powers to the defender'.

The supreme art resides in never losing one's inner calm and in preserving absolute inner stillness. This must be maintained until the movement springs out at the exact moment when the adversary is getting ready to deliver his own blow. That is the great secret of kendō: not so much to attack the man as to assault his mind.

The contest is only a way of making apparent what is already the case. Myomoto Musashi used to say that a fight is always won before it begins. It is first of all won in the mind.

To summarize: a contest must be prepared for well before it begins. Defective preparation of the physical and psychic energies, a hurried plan, or a badly conceived strategy will lead to collapse. Bringing about the collapse of the opponent also depends on a tactic: it is the tactic of 'sticking to the enemy' or entangling him. In other words, overcoming the enemy on his own ground by holding onto his rhythm. This is precisely what the Japanese have done in adapting to Western civilization and surpassing it. One must know the intentions and the methods of the adversary while remaining invisible oneself, for example, by not exporting one's most powerful machines so as not to assist competitors abroad; not revealing one's own methods, but exploiting the adversary's hesitation and acting rapidly. Waiting for the right moment and acting like a bolt from the blue, a basic strategy in martial arts and in Japanese methodology. There must not be a hair's breadth between the moment the attack is decided on and the moment it takes place. Finally, learning to control the adversary by holding to his own rhythm. Modifying this rhythm so as to defeat him in a flash, on the principle that a swifter rhythm always dominates a slower one.

14. The martial arts here and now

Martial arts can be classified, crudely speaking, into three categories: those that are specifically Japanese, or those whose quality restricts their practice to an elite (archery, horseback archery or *yabusame*, *sumō*); those that are popular and have come to be practised all over the world (*jūdō*, *karate*, *aikidō*, *kendō*); and finally, the varied kinds that are practised by a limited number of enthusiasts, (drawing the sword, or *iai*, fencing with a lance, or *naginata*, fighting with two swords, or *nittō*, fencing with a short lance, or *yari*). On the margin of these three main categories there is an extreme variety of arts of attack and defence.

The modern schools (jūdō, aikido, karate, kendō) have gained such popularity that all Japanese practise one or other of these martial arts, in school at least. On the other hand the old schools persist in remote country areas of Japan. Nowadays there are 50 of them at the most, but just like the old samurai, who never touched money, the masters of these schools refuse all profit from their teaching and in each case depend on some other vocation for earning their living. Frequently they are direct descendants of a celebrated samurai.

Until quite recently, there was not merely a prohibition on filming or photographing in these schools, there was a veto on outsiders even being present at the training of the pupils. In the old days, when a master wanted to put the superiority of another school to the test, he would issue a challenge to its master. Then a sword fight might take place. If the defeated party was spared by his adversary, and if he was the one who had thrown down the gauntlet, the ensuing dishonour was so great that he would commit harakiri. This is an indication of the importance of the secret techniques of these schools, techniques which have in many cases disappeared with the death of their last master. As for their deeper teaching, that is given only to the occasional initiate, and even today there is never any question of revealing it.

In the present-day disciplines, all that used to constitute the distinctiveness of the old *bugei* has been polished up and made to conform with our unconscious expectations. There is a copious literature which evokes a rather naive and ingenuous kind of imagery: through thousands of different anecdotes and tales it illustrates the exploits of past and present times. The Japanese themselves are careful not to contradict these or to make any attempt to counter-balance this kind of new romanticism of rivalry and efficiency. Their real message is so remote from anything we are capable of comprehending that they actually use this imagery to protect their secret teaching even more jealously. This is true of Japan not only in the sphere of the martial arts, but in respect of all the traditional ways, including the art of the potters, of the *nō* actors, of the kabuki actors, and of the most diverse kinds of musicians. Behind her ultramodern shop-window, the ancient Japan is silent.

'You Westerners', Takano used to say to me, 'are desperate to understand and explain everything. But in reality, when a man wants to explain what he thinks he has understood, he becomes a prisoner. Words are his prison.' This is the reason why none of the grand masters

ever explain what they know. A pupil must be led to the highest level
of his potential by his inner intuition alone. It is in his mind that
he must act, much more than through his hands. The person who
does become a master captures this harmony as a kind of music that
becomes inherent in his being. This is why a grand master can never
undertake a duel with an opponent while under the influence of rage
or hatred: he must even be above the desire to win or the fear of dying.
His inner state must resemble a calm stretch of water. The sword
that cuts breaks through the disharmony that is before it. It is not
the master who has killed someone, it is the opponent who has just
cut himself open on the master's sword.

Each martial art ultimately conditions a particular morphology,
both physical and mental. Thus, in general we can say that the *sumō*
man is fat, heavy and strong, the *jūdō* man is often tall and robust,
while the *karate* adept is small, thin, taut, and dry.

The art of *karate*, which is certainly the most ancient of all the
martial arts, resides in the ability to turn the fists, and indeed all the
parts of one's body, into a natural strike force.

The essence of *karate*, as of *aikidō*, *jūdō* and of archery, is to avoid
opposing any mental resistance to what is going to happen. The aim
of the training is precisely to bring the pupil to a degree of mental
non-resistance that is akin to a kind of heightened perception. In other
words, the screen formed by habitual mental calculations and reactions
involved in fear or in the simple instinct of self-preservation is so
completely obliterated and the sensation of what is going to be decided
or done by the opponent becomes so immediate and intuitive, that
the riposte arises spontaneously and instantaneously.

Sumō is a very special art and it has not been vulgarized. It has
remained highly competitive. There are in Japan only about 50 great
sumōtori who compete for the championships. These arouse extraordinary excitement and in the largest stadiums the seats are snapped
up well in advance.

The *sumō* fight is a relatively brief affair, it lasts a few minutes at the
most. It consists in hurling the opponent out of a circle traced on
the ground. The assault is therefore exceedingly swift and violent.
The affair begins with the two heavyweights, who often weigh more
than 120 kilos and are more than two metres in girth, swaying like
two huge bears from one foot to the other. Then they crouch down
and greet one another. In competitive bouts, the referee waits until

the two men are breathing at a steady rhythm before he lets them start the fight. This causes incredible suspense, since neither the *sumōtori* nor the spectators in fact know precisely when the signal for the start will be given. With the major championships, it is not unknown for the start to be put back ten times. All the while the two fighters will be staring unblinkingly at each other. Victory will depend on speed of attack.

In actual fact, the teaching of the martial arts in its deepest sense is an initiation into the powers of mind and body. These powers are as limitless as the field of teaching itself. But it is only when a man is inwardly united and liberated that he can also become a true master. He has conquered fear, he is at the centre of himself, he knows within himself a point of equilibrium and a point of energy that he is able to direct. He has therefore gone beyond brute force. He knows how to direct his inner forces, how to use energies other than his purely physical powers. He has definitively gone beyond violence, and this must be why, in the old days, many masters of the martial arts used to become Zen monks.

Nowadays these springs of initiation are drying up in Japan. Nevertheless, Japan's best interests—and perhaps her only real interest, are bound up with these men, who still possess true knowledge— the knowledge which effects an unseen unification and liberation of man.

All these martial arts reflect, as has been said, the purest tradition of the old samurai. In the beginning, fighting techniques were known as *bugei*. They appeared in Japan around the year 700. then in the twelfth century Japanese feudalism was remodelled, and a new social structure emerged under the authority of the shōgun. Now the warrior class was in the first rank of society. These men with a vocation were called samurai, which means servants, vassals, and by extension, soliders. In common speech they were however known as *bushi* (warrior knights). Hence the name of the samurai code: *bushidō*. *Dō* means the way, the path, *bu* the warrior, and *shi* the lord: *bushidō* is thus the collection of rules that tell the samurai how to follow the true way of unconditional obedience to his lord.

15. The spirit of bushidō

Only as recently as 100 years ago, the spirit of *bushidō* still reigned vigorously in Japan. In 1870, when the Emperor Meiji promulgated the decree that abolished feudalism and decided to open his country to the West, the most violent opposition came from the samurai class. To such an extent that for a while the samurai were virtually persecuted. In 1875 the wearing of the sword was forbidden, samurai teaching prohibited and those who defied the law were put in prison. It was not until 1909 that the teaching of the art of the sword, or *kendō*, began again in the university of Tokyo.

The spirit of bushidō persisted. In the course of the last war, the *kamikaze* thus enjoyed the right to wear their samurai sword by virtue of the voluntary sacrifice of their lives. And if the Nipponese soliders in the Pacific fought to the death down to the last man, they did so because it was against the spirit of *bushidō* to surrender.

Today the spirit of bushidō still flourishes in Japan, both in the martial arts and in business, for it is the honour of being the first at any price that motivates a good number of Japanese big bosses.

To love life without ever blinking in the face of death was the first rule of bushidō. It took centuries of struggle and innumerable merciless duels for such a spirit to develop. Combat technique always involves a situation where a man is obliged to defend his life, and has therefore to be stronger than his opponent. This is why the practice of the martial arts teaches efficiency at the same time as forming the inner man.

The practice of the martial arts cannot be dissociated from their religious dimension. All the great masters of Buddhism or Shinto are practitioners—and this fundamental point is too often ignored. It is customary to consider all masters as being essentially inspired by Zen, but in reality, today, practically all the masters of the schools— the *ryū*—are adherents of Shinto.

Nowadays there are several schools of thought among the martial arts. Among them it is however possible to distinguish two major tendencies: one, called *dō*, maintains the spiritual tradition; the other, called *jutsu*, strives chiefly to perfect the art of blows and holds, without reference to rites or traditions. This division is in fact less important than it seems, as there is often considerable difficulty in appreciating to what extent the techniques of *jutsu* are imbued with spiritual qualities. Nonetheless, there is much to be said for a careful study of those schools that have specific roots in the real traditional sources. The more popular the martial arts become, the more they tend to suffer from the predominance of the spirit of competition, a spirit which is like that of modern Western sport, but which is alien to the deeper spirit of *budō*.

16. *The samurai schools*

The true number of Japanese *ryū* (samurai schools) will almost certainly never be known. When an estimate was first made in 1843 by the shōgun, the number of the big schools was reckoned to be 159, of which 61 were for fencing, 29 for bare-fisted combat, 14 for archery, and nine for horse riding, with five other assorted ones. But there were also many clandestine schools, remote little academies, not to mention the fighters called *rōnin*. These fighters were sometimes battle-hardened but without disciples. It was not infrequent for them to take on the masters of well-established big schools on their travels and to defeat them. The superiority of these fighters, perfectly incarnated by Musashi, arose from their continual training and from a practice that had constantly to face up to harsh reality, while the masters of the *ryū* tended sometimes to succumb to the slumber of theory.

It remains nonetheless true that the secret teaching of the ryū has come down to us only in dribs and drabs. What these schools represent is the symbol of an esoteric inward-looking tradition that in some cases survives in our day and in other cases disappeared when certain descendants, on the point of death, destroyed the books and texts left to them by a whole line of masters. These men decided rightly or wrongly that there was no longer anyone worthy of continuing the tradition.

These old martial arts schools have never been the object of detailed study. The secrecy with which they surrounded themselves, a secrecy that still persists today, allows only a very superficial examination. And yet the ryū, buried in the depths of the country, have played a considerable part in the history of Japan. The *ryū* and its masters were often the focus of the whole life of a village. Festivals, tournaments and all kinds of events allowed the villagers to share in the life of the *ryū*. The esoteric aspect of the teaching did not exclude a wide popular expression of it.

The study of these *ryū*, their traditions and the texts and teachings of the masters, would be a source of precious knowledge and would bring to light a Japan that was fascinating and unknown.

When a samurai receives a lesson from the gods or kami

The creation of the oldest school in Japan, the *Katori Shindō Ryū*, seems to have had a typically fairy-tale character. It was the work of Chōisai Iizasa (1387–1488). He was a brave samurai and practitioner of Shinto. One day when he was at the sanctuary of Kashima and Katori, dedicated to Futsu-nushi, *kami* of war, Iizasa had the idea of washing the feet of his horse at the temple fountain. The horse immediately dropped stone dead. Iizasa realized he had just committed a sacrilege. The water of the sanctuary was reserved exclusively for the purification of the faithful. As a sign of penitence, he shut himself up in the temple for a 1000 days, devoting his time to meditation and the art of the sword. He thus had the time to draw up new rules of combat, and the result was the school of *Tensin Sheiden Katori Shindō Ryū*, known as The School of Katori, which he established at the end of his period of penance.

Since then, from father to son, the tradition has continued. Today the heir of the dynasty, called Yasusada, as yet too young and inexpert, is being trained by Otake, who is master of the school at the present time. He has about 1000 followers, spread through the whole of Japan, and less than 30 initiates. The transmission of the secrets is in fact extremely strict. The initiate must sign with his blood (a slight prick of the finger) the promise that he will reveal none of what he has learnt. 'Even the art of pricking the finger is a secret too', master Otake told me with a smile.

The teaching lasts for many years. In the course of the first three years, the pupil must practise the exercises, and at the end of this period he receives the first diploma. Then, three or four years later, he is given a second diploma; and finally, those who manage to reach a certain rank will have the right to receive an initiatory teaching which includes the nine signs necessary for concentration. Meditation is carried out in the *zazen* posture. As for the spiritual teaching, it can be summed up in one sentence: 'If you begin a fight, you must win it,' says master Otake, 'but fighting is not the aim. The warrior's art is the art of peace; the art of peace is the hardest: you must win without fighting.'

The art of the secret

Every school or *ryū* held to the rule of the secret. In the past as today, a science that was divulged was a lost science. The secrecy embraced martial techniques themselves as much as the esoteric teaching. The superiority of a technique could obviously enable a school to survive and could establish the fame of its founder for good. So it was with the establishment of the *Shindō Musō Ryū* (or school of *jūjutsu*). This school went straight into the family of the martial arts, and its importance went on growing, especially during the Tokugawa era, when the tendency to take-on opponents without killing them became increasingly prevalent. Nonetheless, the practice of it remained secret until the Meiji era, and it was only in 1955 that *jūjutsu* lost its warrior form to become another *dō* under the name of *jūdō*. However, many of the schools linked to the *Shindō Musō Ryū* guarded the techniques of *jūjutsu* jealously, while there formed around *jūdō* a federation that was linked to the *kendō* federation.

The education of a samurai: the freedom of extremes
For centuries, the samurai were educated in a tough school. Training began at a very tender age, and it was harsh, often not sparing children the sight of death. At the age of 15 the young samurai received his sword. From then on throughout the whole of his life, he and his weapon would remain bound in an indissoluble friendship.

The education of a young samurai was very full: it was spiritual, physical and technical. The teaching was often oral. A lot of the samurai in the early days of feudalism did not have the time to learn to read and write. Later, the teaching quickly became obligatory. The children were primarily taught Confucianist texts that developed the sense of duty, such as the *Rongo*.

For them, man manifested himself as a unity: earth, heaven and man made into one. The science of energy was above all a science of the communion between man and the Universe. Thus, learning to breathe and to orientate one's breathing meant both learning concentration and learning attentiveness to the points of correspondence between the self and the Universe. The supreme art consisted in developing in oneself a sixth sense that made it possible to gain a spontaneity and a lightning rapidity of reaction in the handling of weapons.

A samurai trained himself to remain alert while asleep so that he was ready to leap up and face any attack. He took his tea squatting on one knee, and with the left hand, so that the right hand was free to reach for the sword in a flash. Horse riding and bowmanship formed part of his essential training, together with bare-fisted fighting and every variety of combat with all kinds of different weapons. The samurai had to be ready to face any situation and be victorious under any conditions.

The sons of the samurai had to get unaided across long steep gorges, and they were spurred to perform the tasks of Sisyphus. Lack of food and exposure to the cold were regarded as highly effective tests to harden them and toughen them up. At the tenderest age, children were sent long distances with messages to perfect strangers: they were made to get up before dawn, read their exercises before breakfast, and go to the master barefoot in the middle of winter.

Quite often (once or twice a month, for example, on the occasion of the festival of the divinities of the science of swordsmanship) they would gather in small groups and go through the night without sleeping, each one taking it in turns to read aloud. Pilgrimages to all sorts of impressive locations (places of execution, cemeteries, houses said to be haunted) were the pastimes allowed to children.

At the time when executions took place in public, not only were the little boys sent to watch the hideous spectacle, but they were sometimes obliged to visit the spot in the middle of the night on their own; all this, of course, to harden them supremely and make them lose all superstition or fear of death. Once they were grown up, most of the samurai behaved with extreme dignity. They for the most part respected the code of honour: the famous *code of bushidō*.

The perfection of the sword and the alchemical science of the swordsmiths
In Japan there are about 900,000 *katana* of all kinds listed in museums, sanctuaries, temples and private collections across the country. Many of these weapons are classed as 'national treasures' or 'important cultural artefacts' and are worth a fortune.

The manufacture of the Japanese sword has, in the course of the centuries, attained to an extraordinary level of perfection. It rests on traditional elements: iron, fire, clay, water and wood—and man himself. The sword is born out of the combination and the quality of these six elements. That is why each sword remains a unique piece; even for the weapons-maker himself, who is by definition incapable of reproducing the same piece exactly.

There are still today a few grand masters who forge on average twelve to thirteen swords a year in Japan. Although the manufacture of a sword requires about two weeks, a period of several months, and often a whole year, will elapse between order and delivery. The master armourer needs a long period of reflection before he decides what model he will forge. For him, the making of the sword remains primarily the expression of an inner harmony: the time, the moment, the conjunction of the planets all play their part. Before setting to work, the master armourer performs ablutions with pure cold water to chase away malign influences. He covers his head with black and puts on clothes of an immaculate whiteness, as a symbol of purity. The overall effect of these rites is to confer a kind of sacrality on the making of the sword.

A sacred mythological origin
It becomes an object that has its own individuality, possessing, as has been said 'a soul', and consequently to be handled with the greatest respect. It should be remembered that the three sacred hidden treasures of Japan are the sword, the jewel (or *magatama*) and the mirror.

The sword is present everywhere in Japanese mythology, folklore and history. Susanoo-no-Mikoto, the son of Izanagi and nephew of the goddess of the Sun Amaterasu, killed the eight-headed dragon and found in its tail the sword that was to become one of the three sacred treasures. This sword (called *Ama-no-murakumo-no-tsurugi*) was kept in the temple of Izumo. On the occasion of a revolt in the province of Suruga, it was handed over to the son of the Emperor Keiko (AD 70-130) to subdue the rebellion. According to legend, the son of the emperor, surrounded by fire in a blazing field, was saved by his sword, which leapt from the scabbard and scythed down the plants around him, creating a way through the flames. This blade was then rebaptised 'the mower of plants' (*Kusanagi-no-tsurugi*).

27. Fire ceremony.

PART 3

3

ECHOES OF THE UNSEEN

1. The soul of Japan: the way of the gods

If there is one overriding reason why we fail to understand the Japanese properly, and why they seem so alien to us, it is their original religion, Shinto.

There are innumerable ways of explaining or defining Shinto. The word itself was not adopted until the sixth century when, in order to define their ancient customs at the time of the increasing diffusion of Buddhism, the Japanese had to find a name to designate the specific character of their own old customs: that name was Shinto, signifying the way of the gods.

Every Japanese, whether he likes it or not, is Shinto before he is Buddhist or Christian. He is born Shinto, just as he dies a Buddhist, quite simply because Shinto venerates life and considers death an impure state. The Shintoists have therefore left ceremonies relating to death to the Buddhists.

In its hieratic and frequently rather disconcerting form, Shinto often seems to a Westerner like the residue of an obsolete animism, and a Westerner may well have difficulty understanding how such an archaic survival can still figure so largely in the life of a sophisticated and hypermodern nation.

There are about 80,000 Shinto sanctuaries in Japan, with innumerable sects more or less closely linked to Shinto and which have over 20,000 temples in the sanctuaries.

One single ritual: purification
Shinto is very simple: there is one single ritual, that of purification. The priest (*gūji*) waves a stick from right to left, and on this stick

are attached jagged strips of paper (*gohei*). It is this stick (*o-harai*) which effects the purification. In addition, purification rites are very widespread outside the sanctuary—particularly purification by water or by fire.

A number of Shinto festivals also involve purification rites. Arrows are sold in a temple and then taken home. There they are laden with all the impurities of the household and burnt at the end of the year in the course of a religious ceremony. Sometimes the arrows brought in by the faithful are purified by the *miko* (or servants of the sanctuary) through their dances. According to another custom, people write or draw their secret desires on little pieces of white paper and these are then thrown into the river by the priests.

Anyone who wants to enter the precincts of a Shinto sanctuary must first purify hands and mouth in water that comes from the fountain. Similarly there is in many Shinto sects a practice of immersing the whole body in the sea at the new year, and this has its origins in the myth of the god Izanagi who, on his return from the underworld, went to purify his body in sea water. Such rites of purification were once much more numerous, and were practised on the occasion of a birth or a death. For Shinto, death creates impurity. That is why the duty of burying the dead is left to the Buddhist religion. Shinto is in fact only interested in life and all the stages of life. Terrestrial life is a happy event. It is a satisfaction desired by the divine spirit.

When a being is purified, harmony is restored in the thing or the place that was troubled, and baneful influences are exorcized.

By extension, a purified being is a new being. The new year, for example, is like a being coming to birth. Old things are burned (purified) either symbolically or in reality, and bad influences are exorcized. Everything must be renewed: man himself—and this is done in the sea—fire, which has to be reborn (the birth of the new fire is brought about by means of the spark that results from the rubbing together of flints or pieces of wood), and this is spirit pouring afresh from matter. The feeling conveyed is that all things are like the waves of an ocean symbolizing eternity. Against this immutable depth all things appear and express an endless becoming. Similarly, purification is the act by which man associates himself with the law of the universe. He creates within himself the harmony of a new body. Anyone who understands this profound instinct finds a way into many hearts in Japan, and sees that country through decidely different eyes.

One single prayer: to make the sound of one's being vibrant
Clap your hands and recite the names of the kami. Clapping one's hands (twice) before the altar of the sanctuary signifies giving a voice to the sound of one's being. One does not address prayers to the kami. To recite their names is sufficient. It is a means of entering into communication with the kami, who know our needs. 'We must reconcile the gods to us and venerate them, but never ask them for anything', said the sage Miyamoto Musashi.

Offerings and festivals: making the kami glad
Before every Shinto altar offerings are placed as nourishment for the kami: sake or rice wine, water, salt, fish, vegetables, fruit.

At the end comes the offering of sake. The sake is drunk spiritually with the kami. Similarly, the innumerable festivals, or *matsuri*, that are held every year in Japan are for the most part organized by Shinto sanctuaries and offered to make the kami glad. Such a notion of respectfulness combined with familiarity towards the kami is hard for us to appreciate. It is somewhat analogous to the veneration occasionally met with in the West for popular saints. Sowing, harvest, an abundant catch, every event of life, are occasions for a festival or a dance. Every temple, every village, every town, every corporation, has its own festival. The spirits of the kami are specially brought out and carried around once a year in sacred reliquaries. It is an honour to carry the heavy reliquary and those who are able to touch the top of it are considered fortunate indeed.

The word 'kami' is untranslatable. A kami is not really a spirit. It is an entity which is fulfilled (or perfect) and which, for this reason, has become worthy not of adoration but of veneration.

The kami are as innumerable as the faces of creation itself. Izanagi-Izanami, the first creator couple, is kami, as is the foremost divinity in Japan: Amaterasu, goddess of the Sun. The kami are an intrinsic part of the 'unseen Japan'; the Japan that is so subtle that it defies explanation.

A common theme in the nation's traditions is that every thing, every being, every manifestation of the living, whether mineral, vegetable, animal or human, possesses a specific quality. This quality is like the seed received before birth. Thus the realization or fulfilment of a grain of wheat will be the ear of wheat. Equally, a small tree can be perfected and become an ancient tree whose branches spread out like a miniature forest. Such a strong and majestic tree may in certain circumstances be venerated. It then becomes kami. It is encircled by a sacred cord (*shimenawa*) which indicates its kami quality. From then on, no-one can cut this sacred tree down. Such trees, with their strings of little cords and paper shapes (*gohei*), are a frequent sight in Shinto temples. It is as if such a tree, in its maturity, has a certain power: or as if it is charged up with a beneficent magnetism. A particularly majestic waterfall like the one at Nachi may also be kami, as may some of the rocks around it.

At Ise, as in numerous Shinto sanctuaries, a white horse is venerated. It is a symbol of purity and knowledge. It is also kami. At first sight, this may provoke a smile. Further thought leads to the reflection that this represents a deep feeling for nature and for the forces of the living, which have a kind of magic power.

As we have said, the kami are numberless, like the numberless manifestations of reality itself.

Amaterasu, goddess of the Sun, is venerated at Ise and at the Meiji sanctuary at Tokyo. She is the symbol of the sun, without which all existence would become impossible. The Emperor is, in a sense, the priest-king of the original goddess.

Ise, most sacred of Shinto sanctuaries

Many emperors have moved their capital and rebuilt it elsewhere from nothing. Numerous temples and castles in Japan have been destroyed by fire more than once and rebuilt in identical form. The idea of such renewal led an emperor to decree in the year 800 that thenceforth, the temple of Ise, first and most sacred of Shinto temples, was to be rebuilt in precisely the same form every 20 years.

The rebuilding of this temple is an event that involves the whole of Japan. The trees have to be fetched from a forest a long way away, a forest that is especially preserved for this sole purpose and cannot be used for anything else. The trees are cut down in accordance with certain religious rites and then brought to the temple site: an atmosphere of festivity and carnival pervades the whole journey.

Despite the apparent simplicity of its construction, the temple of Ise represents an ancient style of architecture that has been preserved down to modern times only as a result of this sacred practice of rebuilding. Teams of carpenters familiar with ancient cutting secrets are trained and kept together for this one purpose. Every Japanese

28. A very old photograph of the most venerable sanctuary in Japan, that of Ise, where Amaterasu, goddess of the Sun, is honoured. It is demolished and rebuilt in identical form every 20 years, as a symbol of renewal. Today, gravel has replaced the long grass. The photograph taken by Edward Sylvester Morse dates from 1880.

will make a pilgrimage to Ise at least once in his life. But no-one goes inside the sanctuary. Only a handful of visitors are granted the exceptional honour of being led before the sacred door of the principal sanctuary and they may approach to within 30 feet of it to pay their respects. The sanctuary is dedicated to Amaterasu, goddess of the sun, and this is where her sacred mirror is kept. It is said that a certain emperor believed himself unworthy to possess such a sacred mirror in his palace, and asked one of his daughters to take the mirror around Japan with her until Amaterasu herself made it plain where she wanted to dwell. After 25 years the emperor's daughter died and another one took her place. It took 50 years of wandering before Amaterasu finally indicated the location of Ise, where she has remained until now. It seems that for centuries no-one has seen this mirror in its hiding-place inside a series of boxes. By tradition the daughters of the emperor are the great priestesses of Ise. They keep watch over the 400 sacred objects (swords) to be found there: no-one is allowed to film or photograph these without express permission, which is rarely in fact ever given.

The reality of Shinto and the unseen Japan
In what way does Shinto express the essence of the Japanese soul?
It reflects a feel for reality, a respect for life, and a sense of pragmatism.
It is an immanent religion, a religion that takes as its starting point
the thousand and one forms of outward reality that constitute the

29. The old and the new. This section of ultra-modern housing is part of
the futurist town that Kenzō Tange would like to build over the Bay
of Tokyo, to accommodate 5,000,000 inhabitants. Kenzō Tange has
written a book on the sanctuary of Ise, and he illustrates the way in
which tradition can remain a source of inspiration.

mirror of the divine. It is the alliance of the two fundamental masculine-feminine principles: Yin-Yang. It is the principle and the alliance of the creator gods or kami: Izanagi (masculine) and Izanami (feminine). Everything that exists comes out of their union. It is a dynamic awareness of the creative principle: Shinto is the religion of the living. Shinto is in fact a very profound philosophy of the qualities and nature of the living.

According to contemporary physics, the quantic universe is essentially what determines fields of energy and interactions between such fields. This is the second level of reality, at which analysis gives way to an 'approximation', at which the observer becomes the observed, at which action and thought are simultaneous. Because of this, Shinto, being linked to the nature of the real, is as ageless as the Real itself. It is infinitely ancient or infinitely modern.

2. The spirit of Zen

The word 'Zen' comes from the sanskrit *dhyāna*, which means meditation. There is a legend that Buddha transmitted its rules to Kâshyapa, his favourite disciple. After this, 27 patriarchs handed down the teaching until Bodhidharma, who came from India to China in the sixth century and was the first Chinese Zen patriarch. Chinese Zen was known as *chan*.

Historically, Zen was introduced into Japan by Eisai in 1192, and again by Dōgen in 1227. Bernard Frank suggests that Zen was an attempt to return to the original rigorousness of Buddhism, in reaction to the simplistic philosophy expounded by Amidist Buddhism. In practice, Zen doctrine exercised a considerable influence in Japan. Its development coincided with the establishment of Japanese feudalism, which dates from the end of the twelfth century. (This marks the time when the class of professional soldiers came into prominence.)

It is easy to say all that Zen is not. It is not a system of ideas, nor a metaphysic, nor a religion. It is not weighted down with dogmas, beliefs, symbols, temples, or monastic vows. For Zen there is nothing to seek nor any merit to be acquired. It is not a way, it does not require any faith, it does not await any saviour, nor does it promise any paradise. It neither offers any choice nor anything to be acquired.

A monk who was the superior of a Zen monastery decided to find a successor. He placed a jug in front of him and asked all the other monks to say a few words in turn about the jug. Each of them struggled to define the jug without seemingly making any impression on the master. The last one to appear was the cook. He scarcely bothered to glance at the jug, but simply gave it a violent kick and shattered it to pieces. Then he turned round and went off. At last the master's face showed signs of approval and it was the cook who was selected.

For Zen this story means that our perceptions are nothing but an illusion. There can be no question of defining the jug, since neither the jug, nor the mind, nor Buddha, nor any being nor any thing have any fundamental reality. That is why in Zen the only dogma, if that term can be employed without paradox, is 'Kill the Buddha'.

First and foremost, Zen is a stone hurled into the lake of appearances to expose the Void of all things. But the ultimate goal pursued by Zen is the essence of the real. Given that this real is the nameless, that is to say the same in essence as the inexpressible and incommunicable Absolute, it is precisely the real that Zen desires to apprehend, beyond any process that might involve the mental or the mode of reasoning with which we are familiar.

That is why Zen does not explain anything. When we define doctrines we make ourselves prisoners of those doctrines, while what is seems like a flash of lightning and disappears as quickly. But the attentive man is able in that very lightning instant to comprehend fleetingly by an illumination known as *satori*.

The idea of the Void can be illustrated thus: if one can conceive the life of man as similar to a knotted cord, Zen proposes, not to add new knots, in other words to multiply his various bonds of knowledge or power, but rather to remove all the knots from the cord, so as to restore it in some sense to its original state of straightness and smoothness. That is why the Zen void is the opposite of nothingness. The Buddhistic sense Zen gives to man signifies that everything already exists in ourselves, and that if only we can get rid of all the things that mist over true knowledge, then we can renew our contact with that knowledge.

It is worth pointing out that a modern physicist is uniquely able to comprehend this reasoning. Ultimately he now knows that no man will ever be able to reconstitute the order of Creation from one fundamental particle. On the contrary, the more the infinitely small is explored, the more numerous are the ever-fresh energy fields that open out in front of us. On the other hand, as everybody knows, the most fantastic energies are to be found on the nuclear level, in other words in the infinitely tiny. In fact the Universe, like the electrons that make it up, is, as Louis de Broglie has put it, no longer anything more than a 'field of probabilities'.

In the order of everyday life, the difficulty is to learn to avoid putting up a screen that conceals what is: when there is no such screen, then movement springs out, the word is spoken, the substance of the real appears. For everyday life, Zen teachers propose an apparently absurd method of meditation that they call the *kōan*. The *kōan* is a formula that cuts across not merely our ways of thought but our whole deep culture, because it tends to reject every kind of intellectual and rational judgement. For instance, a monk was asked the following question: 'How can my hand be like the hand of Buddha?' His reply was: 'You must play the lute in the moonlight'. To the question: 'How can I escape from the word and from silence, since both of them belong to the world of the relative and the absolute?' the reply was given 'I think about the partridges that chatter among sweet-smelling flowers.' In fact such preposterous replies as this from famous monks have given rise to a whole literature of *kōan* that are prescribed material for meditation in the monasteries. But the *kōan* are never anything more than passwords for use in moving from the unreal to the real, intended to bind the disciple to his master. Under the form of an apparently absurd proposition, the *kōan* halts the mental process and its linear logic. For example: 'What noise do you make when you strike the air with only one hand?'

The unity of opposites

In the mentality of Western man, bloated by his rich diet of knowledge, doctrines, and cultures, Zen acts as a violent liberating shock. It requires all activity to cease, it calls for all we have acquired to be rejected and eradicated. For meaning emerges when we stop wanting to explain; progress happens when we stop wanting to make progress. Our cherished notions of effort and progressive striving do not find their full meaning until they cease to be exercised or applied. The focus of pressure is in the direction of offering every opportunity for the will to exert itself, and providing the supreme obstacle against which to struggle. The same is the case with the bow that is excessively taut and difficult to handle. When we cease to want to progress, that which is tension becomes freedom, that which is constraint becomes

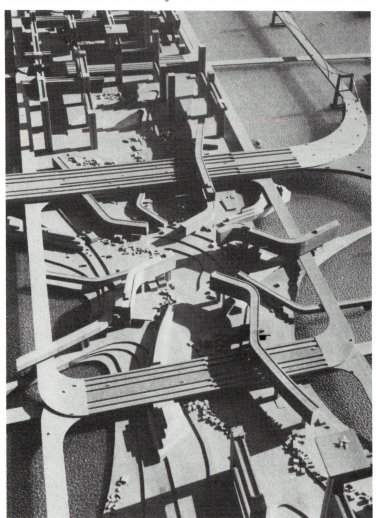

30. Kenzō Tange's overriding preoccupation is the relationship between man and his architectural environment. He has designed a futuristic city which operates on three levels. He has conceived the main highway which crosses the bay of Tokyo as being analogous to the human spine. The relationship between the areas assigned to working and living has been worked out in such a way as to provide a vision of the homogeneous city, the interdependence of each section functioning as part of an organic whole, and the expression of a unified social, cultural and creative philosophy.

joy, effort becomes non-effort. A person perceives that he contains within himself that which he was desperately seeking elsewhere or that which he was despairing of ever managing to grasp.

Many Zen masters have done obeisance to that minor art, the art of writing. They have always managed to practise it with inimitable humour. Words are only materials that can be used to short-circuit habits of thought, to make thought slough off its habits. Their stories are invariably like the farce of the chair that is pulled away at the last moment, and this is a way of demonstrating that there can be no certainty.

Zen and the samurai

How can we reconcile the violent art of war with the non-violence, detachment and peaceableness of Zen? How did Zen somehow become the fundamental ethic of the samurai?

The paradox is easily explained. A samurai is above all a man who, in the face of the idea of death, must go beyond both the desire for life and the desire for death, for the two aspects are each a product of illusion. Above all, Zen teaches a courage beyond courage and a faith beyond all mysticisms and pamperings of the soul. The rigour of Zen suited the implacable life of the samurai.

Thus Zen is expressed equally well in the martial arts, in the art of flower arranging, in the tea ceremony, or in calligraphy. Just as all reality is spontaneous, Zen strives to give expression to reality itself and to all that is, and it springs up in a flash. It can be applied equally to expression of artistic, poetic, practical, and religious life.

The spirit of Zen teaches that when a man does what life intends him to do, when he does it as well as he can, and provided he is free of all fear, then the infinite is realized in him. Such a spirituality beyond all faith or religious dogma, a realization of one's being beyond all reasoning and all controversies of the intellect, has of course proved an attraction to some of the best minds among the western intelligentsia. The great certainty of Zen is that there is nothing to seek. The person who perceives within himself the relationship that binds him both to the world of the infinitely small and the world of the infinitely great is like a drop of water carried away on a river and lost in the immensity of the ocean. This drop of water has neither desire nor revolt, it is unique and yet at the same time it is lost in the midst of the totality of water. This is a state of being that eludes all verbal expression; Zen wants to convey it without recourse to definition.

Westerners have too much culture, they lose sight of what is essential. Talking about Zen is as absurd as wanting to analyze one's own heartbeat. Zen can be summed up in the simple proposition: What is, is.

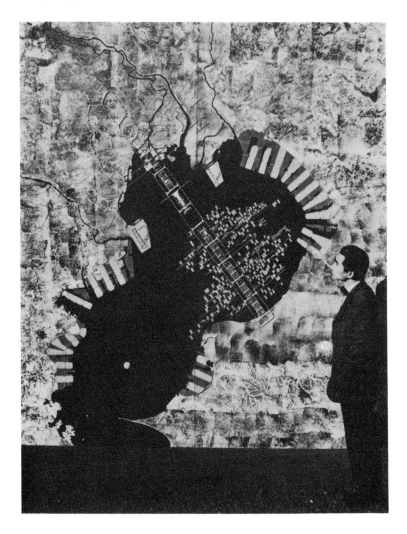

31. Kenzō Tange in front of the model of his futurist town. 'Tell me where you are looking and I will tell you who you are.'

32. Kazuo Suhara, one of the grand masters of Zen, in the temple of Kamakura.

The whole of Zen literature, its poetry and its stories amount to a repetition of this in a thousand and one different forms. It is extraordinary that the most difficult thing to accept is the evidence. But what matters is to appreciate how it can benefit us. Given that all we imagine to be reality is not and cannot be reality, given that the structure of our minds and the influence of our feelings creates illusory and phantasmagorical forms which come from within us and in their turn reflect ourselves indefinitely as in a game of mirrors,

33. Professor Kenichi Fukui, awarded the Nobel prize for chemistry, seen here photographed in his office, says 'Reality is "holistic".' Master Suhara says 'Reality is the vibration of thought'. At the frontiers of knowledge the mind, whether engaged in scientific research or inner self-discovery, encounters the fundamental unity that underlies everything.

then we can allow ourselves to enjoy peace of mind. We must stop identifying ourselves with our definitions. The calm and liberated mind can then grasp the true nature of the real. The paradox is that although we cannot express the nature of things, we do have the possibility of feeling what they are, without any other form of analysis. Though incapable of defining concepts such as eternity or the infinite,

I can still become aware of them myself in profoundly indefinable perceptions.

Consequently, when I am freed from all identification, whether profane, sacred or confessional, I am free today: 'Kill the Buddha!' If I am freed from any dogmatic thought, I can say: 'The way which is the way is not the way', or 'the name which is the name is not the name'. After all, Heisenberg himself showed us that we cannot observe the real without modifying the nature of this real, quite simply because we are always a cause and a part of this real.

Zen simply places the individual on the edge of the sword and tells him: 'Go on. If you are afraid, you will be cut; if you stay calm, you will be able to dance on the blade'. In practice, this can also mean keeping imperturbably cool in the moment of greatest danger. We can behave like the Zen monk who found himself in a coach whose brakes had just failed while it was going down hill. He remained peaceful and calm in the midst of the general panic and confusion. When the coach eventually came to a miraculous stop, the others crowded round him. 'How did you manage to keep so calm' they asked him. 'Because I was watching for the best moment to jump', he replied.

The reason that Buddhism, and Zen in particular, were, unlike Christianity, able to establish themselves easily in Japan without encountering resistance, is that Buddhism and Shinto were ultimately complementary. Buddhism gave Shinto, which was a religion of local customs, a wider extension, a universal dimension. It brought to Shinto the metaphysical and philosophic framework that it lacked.

3. The impermanence of things and the quality of being

Style and the flower
Style (*fū*) is what characterizes the role of an actor. The Japanese mind always looks for an overall vision. The body and the landscape of the body 'flower' appear in harmony. The *flower* is the essence of all things. According to Zeami, 'A modest nō actor, who strives consistently to understand and perfect his *métier* succeeds in knowing the "*flower*" . . . he will keep the flower until he is very old. And that because he has known nō from the very beginning. If a person builds on this knowledge of nō to meditate deeply, he

will be able to recognize the seed of the *flower*.'*

We would say today that the flower is born of non-separability. The consistent aspect of reality blurs its complex aspects. A number of elements make up one and the same element, whether we are doing a very small thing or something highly skilled like turning a vase. But to succeed in creating a vase, a person must carry each of the states and moments of that creation to its purest expression. All *presences*, all states of conscience are 'flower' in some sense. The ultimate realization is flower, for it unites and conjugates with all these non-separated states.

This is what the Zen master Suzuki Shoshan says in reference to some lines from an old poem:

> Wakening is the wakening that wakes without waking
> The waking that wakes is awakening in a dream.

There is no awakening of that which is. But not to be awake to that which is means the death of the awakening (thus of reality).

Visualizing reality

What is a circle? It is a symmetrical reality. Every point is at an equal distance from the centre. But the circle is already the representation of a point, and is itself only the extension of a point. Thus the image of the circle is at once absolute and perfect, but it does not reflect the dynamism of the living. The dynamic figure is the spiral. Something that unwinds and becomes and is never the same. The spiral inscribes the endless interplay of forms and plans that are for ever different, even though they are linked to the centre.

Every local movement is a gesture that can be extended into infinity. The open palm of the Buddhas represents the Extended, the Infinite. A closed fist represents only itself. If nothing is separated, the smallest sound or the smallest gesture evolves and can be visualized in its cosmic totality. A point is infinitely small or infinitely great, like the immense Universe which is still only a point. Such is the secret. This may seem completely visionary or idealistic to us. But if those are indeed the properties of the Universe, if 'non-separability' is, one might say, a physiology, an organic mode of functioning of the Universe, what better way could there be of expressing and representing it?

* *Secret tradition of nō* , p.101.

Everything looks different once we stop seeing a particular thing and visualize our destiny. Everything we do contains our whole destiny. But in relation to all the events of his life a man is at one and the same time committed and free. In this sense every rigid or dogmatic attitude is a false attitude.

> What divine thing
> Can deign to be there?
> I do not know. And yet
> My tears overflow
> Through my being imbued with grace.

These verses by the poet-monk Saigyo, who lived in the twelfth century, express all the inexpressible tension of reality: What is, exists. It is the ultimate appeal of what is, a supreme grace. And what is the nature of that supreme grace? I do not know. But reality exists, it is at one and the same time harmony and disharmony. This situation implies a space between two things, like a distance which is both separation and union. That which unites also separates, that which separates unites. Tension means the actual forces of the living; it is through tension that things are born and the alchemists' transmutation is accomplished: that is nothing other than the expression of the dynamic forces of life; the famous negentropy, to use scientific terms. Tension is again Zen's dynamic of contraries, or the manifestation of reality itself in all its forms.

That which is, is comparable to a point. A point is limited neither in its infinite smallness nor in its infinite greatness. Whatever its dimensions, our universe is only a point. All that is manifested within this point exists. Such existence is here relative, relative to the form of things, to their situation in space-time. Beyond it there is still a state of being that does not relate to any tension and does not come between any extremes, for it cannot be manifested by anything. We will simply say that *that is*.

Again, this being is not a dimension that we can evaluate, measure or calculate. Nor is it a situation of things, or of reality, that we can ignore. It was perfectly comprehensible that the traditional thought of the poet, the philosopher, and the Japanese spirit of 'finesse' should make of this 'being' of things a fundamental reality, in comparison with which all the rest is nothing but disorder.

It is equally comprehensible that contemporary physics should be discovering increasingly subtle properties of reality, to the extent of going beyond any concept of an object and adopting the idea of fields of pure energy. Now such fields are similar to thought. Form-thoughts that are more and more finely-textured merge in their ultimate purity with the very being of reality. A 'being' that really has nothing to do with the multiplicity of forms or infinite complexity.

> The perfect way is without difficulty,
> Except that it avoids choice.
> It is only when you cease to love or hate
> That all can be clearly understood.
> A minute difference
> Suffices to divide heaven from Earth.
> If you wish to attain to the lucidity of truth,
> Do not concern yourself with the just and the non-just.
> Conflicts over the just and the non-just
> Are the malady of the spirit.
>
> Seng Can, *Xinxin Ming*

The serenity of harmony or the state of mushin

The state of *mushin* means that I abandon and leave behind my knowledge and all that I consider such, in the cloakroom. The state of a mirror that sees a mirror, that looks at the mirror looking at it, is always and again my self. The self is as cumbersome as it is useless. It is always involved in all my actions like a bothersome intruder or an importunate visitor. Access to reality is prevented by the self. Furthermore, I do not have any precise idea what the self is.

This means I must let go, I must abandon the self and the pleasures and sufferings that come from it. This is difficult, no doubt. But passion is beyond passion. True passion consists in realizing the depths of my being, it is the passion of a journey to the roots, analogous with the journey to the heights. From the point where I stand, there is no longer either root or summit, past or future. My state of mind is untranslatable. It is the state of the non-mental, a state without ideas and without thoughts. *Mushin* also signifies an emptiness of heart. Sometimes this word is found reinforced by a similar word: *munen-muso*. The suffix *mu* expresses negation and repetition.

Reality possesses all the qualities I desire, my self possesses all the limitations of the ego. In harmonizing myself with reality I make myself transparent; openness to reality is precisely a state without intentions or ideas. I leave aside mental activity for the sake of *ai*, harmony and purification. *Mushin* implies serenity. *Mushin-ni-nemuru* signifies sleeping serenely. This state of inward serenity (*seihitsu*) is like a bottomless transparency. The greater the degree of abstraction from the mental, the more bottomless the serenity. To live the clarity of reality is to accentuate one's consciousness of the real. To this extent *mushin* considerably expands the field and the potential of what we perceive as real.

The soul and the underlying awareness of things: tama

Shinto has a word to express an essence that is at once natural and sacred and worthy of veneration: it is the word *tama*. *Tama* is the spirit, the soul. But it is the union of soul or spirit or consciousness with things that creates nature, or rather that gives to the substance of each thing its true nature, its true corporeity. *Nigi-mitama* is the spirit brought to union and harmony. *Kushi-mitama* is the spirit that leads to mysterious transformations. *Tama* essentially expresses the essence of a thing and a being. An essence which is sacred by nature and reveals its sacred nature by the relation of being to being or of being to thing.

Ma: The secret of space and time

The comprehension of space-time is a deep secret. Space-time is in some sense our sensorial clothing. All our actions, all our perceptions and thoughts are tributaries of space-time. The Japanese define space-time by a single word: *ma*. *Ma* designates a space or an interval between two things. The secret of secrets in the struggle between two adversaries resides in the true perception of the interval between them, or the *mahai*. *Mahai* is at once perception and strategy, tactics and rhythm, *mahai* is comparable with a living field in which all the faculties of being are awakened to their highest degree. This field is both extremely precise and as undefinable as a wave. The person who has such perception knows instantaneously in the tenth of a second how to react to an attack, that is to say how to anticipate an attack before it even happens, and there is time for his sword to cut into an enemy with lightning speed. A good example of *mahai* and the mastery of it is given by Ueshiba, founder of aikido. Whatever his position, whether he was seated, lying down, or on his back, anyone who closed up on him for an attack would inevitably find himself thrown headlong.

34. Gable of the great Olympic stadium at Tokyo, by Kenzō Tange. Once again traditional forms can be seen to have provided the inspiration for the construction of the roof and principal cable. The three concrete struts recall the crossed wooden beams, or *Chigi*, of Shinto Sanctuaries. A design based on the form of the spiral gives the roof its thrusting dynamism.

In Japan, everything always comes down to *ma*, space. The art of fighting, like architecture, music or the art of living, aesthetics, the sense of proportion, the planning of a garden always all depend on a body of meanings which are bound to each other and depend on each other as a function of *ma*. Even a personal contact between two businessmen in Japan is subject to the same concept of *ma*. Here, it is a question of sensing how one's partner assesses things. Space will express itself as hierarchy in the matter of choices, as priority in the sphere of investments, as time and rhythm in the organization of the company and in the perception of men and situations. *Ma* underlies all things, it is the indefinable space that is like the musical harmony of each thing, the right interval and the best resonance.

Japanese space is always bound up with this sublimation of the void. For in order to live in a given space with the greatest possible liberty, we must first of all create void. Then the void will be occupied

35. Cathedral of St. Mary, Tokyo, by Kenzō Tange. Great beauty of line combined with an exterior cladding which picks up and reflects even the smallest amount of available light.

in some way. But the vibration of the void and the 'presence' of the void must remain perceptible. This is the key to understanding Kenzō Tange's work, which includes some of the finest architectural achievements of today. Although modern cities in Japan bear more than a little resemblance to giant meccano kits, this is only a result of the astonishing rapidity with which the Japanese have built their towns. Urban space is the image of a chaos that is provisionally organized. But solutions do exist. Thus, Kenzō Tange wants to build a new Tokyo on the pattern of Ise, a town that will have five million inhabitants and will stand in the sea, in the bay of Tokyo.

The power of Wa

Wa is a Japanese word for the two concepts of harmony and 'communion'. It is also the original name for Japan itself, which was known as 'the country of Wa', or 'country of peace'.

It is this power of *Wa* which is the power and the voice to be found under the innumerable forms of Japanese culture. It is applicable to the tea ceremony as well as to the art of gardens, to flower arranging as well as to calligraphy, to the nō theatre as well as to the Zen art of archery. This secret power of communion and harmony is not definable, it simply is.

Giri: the sense of duty, right behaviour, and spiritual transmission

In Japan, the art of living implies continuity. To perpetuate from father to son the family and the essence of one's ancestors, is to respect the central tree that binds all men to the original kami: the creator couple Izanagi-Izanami. This continuity is in fact a form of respect for life, for oneself and also for one's ancestors. The art of it lies in the quality of the transmission. This transmission is not always consanguinous. If a son does not match up to expectations, or if there is no heir, transmission is effected by the adoption of a spiritual heir. The masters of martial arts, the potters, the artisans and the samurai collectively all obey this same rule.

The corollary resides in the veneration of ancestors. The veneration of the dead is part of life and above all of the respect we owe to ourselves. The dead know our needs. If we invoke them they answer us.

Giri signifies 'duty', 'uprightness' or 'rectitude'. These are obligatory for those who respect personal honour. Each class of the population and each Japanese in particular is subject to a particular *giri*.

The higher a person rises through the ranks of society, the more demanding the *giri*. The code of the samurai included a *giri* exalting honour and therefore life itself. At the level of the pupil and the student, duty consists in passing exams. In cases of exam failure, *giri* is sometimes the cause of suicide.

The wisdom of forms

There is probably no other country in which harmony of forms expresses a wisdom of thought to the extent that it does in Japan. Wisdom means the unrestrained association of man with his nature. As a general rule, it is the most elementary forms that are the most sought after; whether a temple is Shinto or Zen, the wood used to build it will be as pure and as natural as possible. Purity of line is also a purity of mind. The heart is in harmony when it is indwelt by the vibration of real things.

Nature is the real mirror. Limpid water is equally the mirror of a woman and that of the sky. It is youthfulness and freshness. It is what polishes and gives back to man his original virginity. It is the eternal return to the springs of inner clarity. All the natures of the invisible are reflected in water. The mysterious association that the Japanese are able to make between water, rocks and lights gives an indefinable feeling to their gardens. Beauty creates beauty endlessly and renews it like a series of reflected mirror images.

Nature is always surprise, spontaneity and invention. The Japanese garden has not the slightest symmetry, for it weds and organizes asymmetry, as an equilibrium between order or harmony and the rupture of that harmony.

All things have a meaning, each thing is a beginning, a starting-point, underlined by a branch, a tree, a stone. We would say that in a non-local situation, that of quantic vibration, man has need of a local point, of some reference to the first degree of reality. But this first degree is always there without being there totally. It also has its secret. Every point, every rock, every hollow tree, every spring is also a centre around which is organized a series of correlations integrating it into a temple, a sanctuary, or a palace. Witness the imperial villa of Katsura at Kyōtō, where the whole architectural ensemble is closely involved with the vibration of the garden.

When the master of the tea ceremony dips his delicate bamboo spoon in the kettle, he listens to the water, he listens to the sound of

36. Kenzō Tange: facade of the Sōgetsu building at Tokyo. A moving tableau
in which nature is reflected, a quasi-surrealist flight in which space creates
space.

waves and sea made by the water (for as it boils, it lifts a piece of
metal on the bottom); he breaks the harmony of the water for a
moment in order to pour the essence of it as a delicate beverage into
the teapots and to bring together the harmony of the water, the
harmony of the tea chamber and inner harmony. Thus we can
understand why the tea Chamber is called the Chamber of the Void.

The awakening of the soul, the presenting of the taste and savour of things, such is the meaning of all Japanese art. The art of the garden, whether in a vase or over a larger surface has no other aim than this.

The stone is not just any object, it is a living thing, toughened and polished by time, and as a rule it is not worked on by human hands, except for the purpose of emphasizing some natural form. Without question, the stone is the ornament that is the most prized and the most central in every Japanese garden. The stone is the locus of a localization, it embodies a natural magic. A man can know this magic by entering into an alliance with the stone or the tree or the mountain. Everywhere life is infused with life, everywhere the sacredness of forms is clothed with a familiar sacrality. Being is perpetually nourished by nature, not through indifferent contemplation, but through harmonization in a reciprocal communion. From this communion are born art and the comprehension of all things.

Mie-gakure: 'Seen and hidden'

In the famous Ryōan-ji garden in a Zen temple at Kyōtō there are 15 rocks. But no matter where you stand to look at them, there is always one that is hidden. At a given moment, the fifteenth rock becomes visible, while another vanishes.

This is an illustration of the whole working of reality. That which seems continuous is also discontinuous. All that is of space is also of time. But the two are, and are not, both at the same time. Space and time exist, but they are also relative to our scales of measurement and our perception.

The rebuilding of the great temple of Ise every 20 years does not simply express the concept of renewal. A temple is by definition what it is at Ise—the place that contains the sacred treasures. These treasures express the soul of things. And this soul is revealed the better the more it is hidden. The force of things depends on them possessing a 'within the within'. This within is the absolute energy of all reality as long as it remains invisible.

The 'immutable pillar of the heart'

In the void space of the Shinto sanctuary at Ise, under a tiny little miniature roof, can be seen the 'immutable pillar of the heart'.

Each temple at Ise includes two sites: one is the location of the void and the absence, the *Kōdenshi*: the other is full, it is the location of the presence. The divine seems to be present and absent at the same time. According to Tadao Takemoto, the 'honourable pillar of the heart' that is sunk into the middle of the *Kōdenshi* represents the key to this symbol. He says 'it could be compared with a navel. This is the zero point from which springs the sacred'.

The Japanese house has a roof that is built before the walls, and it rests entirely on a central pillar. This pillar is the axis around which will emerge the codified and harmonious forms. It is both a springing forth and an axis that holds all together. The pillar must be lined up very carefully; a tree always stands in the line of its roots reaching up to the sky. An inverted pillar would signify that the house possessed maleficent qualities in which the fields of energy would be contrary.

The garden of sounds and music

The Japanese have a habit of hanging little bells up in their gardens and attaching rectangular pieces of paper to them. Life is thus subtly impregnated with the continual jingling of these little bells as they are rocked by the breezes.

There are sensible people in Japan who will tell you that in their country there are specific 'musics' with innumerable instruments corresponding to each of them: they say there is a Shinto music, a Buddhist music, a court music, a theatre music, etc. And then we could discuss the endless types of popular music, with all their variations from one province to the next. But the most striking thing about the musical tastes of the Japanese is their inordinate predilection for every variety of drum, tamborine and flute. The best known and the most formidable of these flutes, which could once be used as a weapon, is the *shakuhachi*, cut out of very tough and knotty bamboo.

Dances, religion, feminine cults and good humour have all been bound up together with music since the very earliest days in Japan. The goddess of the Sun, Amaterasu, was so weary of the endless facetiousness of her cousin Susanoo, that she hid away in a cave. Immediately the world was plunged into darkness and affliction. Gods and goddesses gathered at the mouth of the cave and one of the goddesses began to dance naked—to the great amusement of the assembled deities. Amaterasu was intrigued to hear so much laughing and put her head outside the cave, whereupon the gods dragged her out and put an enormous rock in the entrance. So it was that the world could once more enjoy the sun and know real *joie de vivre*.

There is a remarkable gaiety in Japanese villages. Throughout the year there are numerous festivals either in honour of the kami or to celebrate fertility rites, the new year, the changing of the seasons, etc. All these are very merry festivals. Assorted groups wander the streets of the villages, banging with all their might on massive drums (*ō-daiko*) or on all kinds of flat drums (*taiko*), to the accompaniment of melodies on a six-holed flute made from a simple strip of bamboo (*take-bue*).

In general the Japanese are very fond of pure sounds, such as are made by clapping, rubbing or percussion with very simple objects: wooden pieces or sticks, bamboo canes, gongs or different types of bronze or metal surface. The main thing for them is to listen to the sound that is produced in this way, to allow it to express all its fullness. In this way the sound creates and prolongs a state of being. Strangely, when such states of being have been experienced, they stay alive in the memory for a long time afterwards, like diffuse and imponderable sensations. The sound of shrill, strident, melodious or cacophonous flutes has often accompanied me in my visits to Zen temples or Shinto sanctuaries.

It is difficult to give any detailed account of these musical instruments, because they are so numerous. Even the best-informed among the Japanese themselves cannot be familiar with all of them. Moreover, there are many instruments that can no longer be used, since the ancient musical scales have ceased to be comprehensible; no-one nowadays knows how to play them.

However, you will easily find a friend who knows some marvellous master of the *shakuhachi*, a lady who is skilful at playing the *koto* or the *shamisen*, two very famous stringed instruments. Ask them to play a few notes on the *kokin*, a two-stringed instrument, or on the *kokyū* (with four strings), for their full vibrato is only heard very rarely nowadays.

Nor must we forget, when speaking of the Japanese garden of music and sound, to include those unforgettable *miko*—girls dressed in red and white who serve the Shinto priests. During the ceremonies and dances it is they who shake the *suzu*, which is a collection of 11 little bells mounted on a branch. There is a special charm in the freshness of the *miko*, the sharpness of the little bells, and the grave or raucous voices of the Shinto priests as they chant the names of the kami.

There was a custom among the samurai of walking around playing the flute on the eve of terrible battles. Life and death, the indefinable, the impermanence of things and beings: all is music. The wind, the waters, the leaves that fall, the sounds of the forest: that music too will be heard and repeated with a solemnity, a melancholy and a rhythm of beings and things that remains unforgettable.

The tea ceremony

It is very hard for those who have not experienced it, to conceive what the tea ceremony can really be like in Japan. And yet, what could be more banal than to prepare and drink a cup of tea? I never really understood what the tea ceremony could mean until one day I was allowed to be present at the real thing in Tokyo. Our hostess, madame Okumura, a follower of the *Ura Senke* school of the art of tea, was waiting for us in the ceremony room, with knees crossed underneath her. There was a tatami floor, the architecture was soberly conceived in white wood and in the centre of the room was a drawing in Chinese ink with a little bouquet beneath it. On the left were two girls, both kneeling. Next to them was a little heap of wooden coals painted white. These would be used to boil water in a container resting in a little square hole in the floor. We waited in silence while the water began to boil. Then the girls used a beautiful wooden ladle with a long slender handle to draw out the water. Each gesture was infinitely leisured and deliberate. The water was poured into a stoneware bowl, which contained a little green powder, the special kind of tea used exclusively for this ceremony. Water and powder were mixed together with a wooden whisk made from delicately cut strips. Then the girls bowed low to each other before passing the bowls to the guests.

Such a brief description totally fails to do justice to the atmosphere generated by this ceremony. It took no less than two hours from beginning to end. Throughout this time no-one spoke a word. The gestures necessary for the preparation of the tea merely added further weight to the silence. Perhaps it would be appropriate to use the word 'contemplation' here.

As I was leaving at the end of the ceremony, I put a question to one of the girls who had served us: 'How long have you been learning the tea ceremony?' 'I have been doing two sessions a week for ten years', she said. 'But how can you possibly spend ten years learning gestures that can be mastered in a much briefer space of time?'

'Because the thing that has to be discovered is an inner reality', she replied.

I must add that there was such a grace and such a beauty emanating from this girl that a French television cameraman who was with me was moved to say: 'That's the first time I have looked at a woman without getting ideas.'

I have had the privilege of interviewing the President of the Ura Senke school, master Sōshitsu Sen, direct descendant of Rikyū, the greatest of all the tea masters, who lived in the sixteenth century.

'Master', I said, 'to what extent does the tea ceremony give expression to Zen?'

'It's a very long story', he said, 'It goes back to the Nara period, around the seventh century'.

In other words, when Buddhism was introduced into Japan for the first time. But it was above all in the Kamakura period, around the thirteenth century, that the Buddhist priests went to China to study Zen thought. When they came back they brought with them not only Zen thought, but the tea ceremony, which they established at this period.

'To what extent is it true to say that the tea ceremony involves a spiritual quest?'

'At the heart of the tea ceremony is a meeting of souls. There are not hosts and guests separately. In a tea pavilion you find a communion of souls, that is to say an intersubjectivity.'

'Is there some search for inner perfection through the perfection of the gestures?'

'The chief signification of the gesture is self-training; thus all the gestures must contribute to the perfection of oneself first and foremost. Through this search for self-perfection, one manages to confront or greet others perfectly. To begin with there is the search for oneself that means one opens up to others in a kind of communion.'

'Do you think that Zen, and especially the tea ceremony, could become popular in the West and in France?'

'It is true that modern men are searching for some such way to rediscover their inner world. In Zen and the tea ceremony they can rediscover what they have lost in their civilization.'

'Master, can we attain to *satori* through *cha-no-yu*?'

'Yes, you can attain to *satori* by following the way of the tea ceremony. But there is no difference, since in Zen they give the *kōan*, that is to say a question, and the question is a focus for meditation; the result would be *satori*. There are two different ways of attaining *satori*, and one goes through static meditation, the other through movement. *Satori* is a state in which there is a complete lack of resistance towards those whom you meet. It is a state of perfect liberty and through the tea ceremony there is a striving for this state.'

The tenderness of the implacable

Winning the friendship of the Japanese means discovering the level at which they are seemingly most contradictory; the level at which serenity and compassion coexist, along with self-mastery and the dionysiac spirit. The distant shamanic past is always there. The spirit of the festival too. Drinking and laughing, the companionship of pretty girls and the pleasures of relaxing with friends are also a part of the Japanese tradition. These are the moments when the natural finds expression, when good taste manifests itself in gaiety. Drinking, yes, but self-mastery in the midst of the drinking: laughing and sharing, these are fine too, in their consensus of good humour and pleasure, as long as no-one lapses into vulgarity. Celebrating, yes, without being starchy, but naturally, always being oneself, whatever one does for the pleasure of being together and sharing.

The expression of wild passion also has its place in Japan. Japanese films are an excellent illustration of those mechanisms of cruelty and implacability, that terrible mirror in which man sees himself driven to the worst extremes. And yet even here the victory goes to the one who does not lose his self-mastery even in the most testing conditions.

In the art of Hokusai the calm sea becomes like a terrible tiger. With one wave it leaps and engulfs the boat. Avenging phantoms and spirits, the souls of the dead, the most remote of superstitions all make up this extremely complex soul in which everything is present, without anything ever being clearly expressed.

Although forms exist, only the unseen is real. Likewise the hidden feeling is always the decisive one. The strategy is always Machiavellian, and yet it is nothing if not sincere. Even if the opponents are unevenly matched, a Japanese will carry on fighting right up to the end. He expects to find an equal determination in us; then the tables may be turned. Living is the art of a tension.

Nothing exists except this tension, this will to be, this veiled calm of contained energy. That in a way expresses and symbolizes the whole secret of strategy in Japan. An invisible key that is yet perpetually present, as are all the Japanese forms themselves. A perfection, a rigour, a harmony, a secret beauty. The sword is the perfected image of this double-edged tension. It expresses the tension of the accomplished work, the sacred sense of life and death, and the very essence of lightning attack. It is difficult to say whether we can share in such a sensitivity, and indeed whether we can even really understand it. But it is the sensitivity of the Japanese people, and we have the task of tracing the unvarying presence of this unseen face, a kind of creative code, smiling yet implacable.

4. Conclusion

The Byzantines of the Mandala

This thesis that Japan remains 'hard and pure' in the face of one and all is naturally open to criticism. The terms are associated with the worst period of Japanese militarism, and nowadays they no longer seem appropriate. And yet the monolithic attitude of the Japanese to the external world has never really changed. Japan looks like a prodigious western-style shop-window, and her expansive power impels her to invade the whole world. But in reality, Japan remains almost as hermetic and closed as in the era of the Tokugawa or the Heian period.

I have presented a very crude picture of Japan, without attempting to indicate the multiplicity of nuances encountered in reality. But Japan functions like a multi-national corporation without a public relations department. The foreigner in Japan, whatever his love and appreciation for the culture, spirit, and qualities of the Japanese, finds no lack of evidence that they are not really interested in him.

So many allegedly international conferences are held where only the names of the foreign participants are listed. The names of the Japanese conferees are not even translated into a Western language.

The Tokyo Underground destination boards have only recently begun to include an accompanying English rendering. In fact it is quite impossible to travel in Japan without some knowledge of Japanese or without the services of a guide. Even at the Tsukuba Exhibition, the foreigner has trouble getting information. This leads to endless loss of time and perpetual misunderstandings. Generally speaking, that knack for relationships and delicacy which has in fact historically been at the heart of Japanese tradition, is completely lacking in modern Japan. Strong in the strength of her particular qualities, insular Japan remains very inward-looking. Anyone who has lived in the country for even a very short time knows how difficult, how onerous, and how time-consuming everything is there. There is a distinction to be drawn between Japanese international expansion and the meaning of her international relations. It is true that the inner depth of Japan is untranslatable, and that the West is deformed by a dualism not found in Japan. It is true that we are presented with the confrontation of two absolutely opposed cultures: one embodying all the terms that we can group under the word 'integration'—globalization and homogeneity in all aspects of social, religious, economic, and political life: the other embodying everything to do with 'disintegration'—that is to say the decline of the West into analytic fragmentation.

This might be expressed by contrasting the symbol of the mandala with that of the machine. The mandala remains as it is in itself, immutable. It symbolizes the permanent quality of the real. The machine is precarious, multiple, and eminently changeable. The two concepts in fact stand over against each other, and one of them must eventually triumph over the other. All action in whatever domain takes time in Japan. The old rule is still there and it says that the sword that cuts quickly does not cut at all. It is the rule of 'slow, slow: quick, quick' that prevails. Japanese strategy is self-assured and master of itself, and it never loses its centre. Following the famous strategist Shingen, we can say that in a battle the mastery goes to the one who never loses his centre whatever the dangers: the mountain that does not move. The result is that the Japanese advance seems irresistible as long as Japan herself remains definitively closed.

And yet no matter how valid the Japanese attitude may be, no monolithic situation is ultimately a solution to anything. The Japanese are pushing the West back on itself like a boomerang. They are certainly curious about what the Westerners think of Japan and they are happy to translate some of the innumerable books and articles that are published on their country. By contrast, you can search as hard as you like for analogous works by Japanese writers on what the Japanese think of the Americans, the Germans, the Italians or the French; you won't find a single one, apart from the multitude of confidential economic theses and studies.

Once the curiosity and the fascination have died down, such an enormous disparity may give rise to xenophobia and rejection. Where is the borderline between Japanese politeness and disdainful arrogance? Why should Japanese ostracism of the West not provoke rejection by the other side? This is a very important question, given that over and above the question of interests, the emotional factor is primordial not only in Japan but in the West as well. A rejection of Japan might all too easily become a rejection of traditional values, with all their infinite riches. Yet do we not have a great deal to gain by seeking inspiration from this most remarkable aspect of the Japanese model? Every 'pure and hard' strategy inevitably provokes an analogous response. What would be the use of a moribund West exculpating itself by making Japan the scapegoat for all its ills? What would be the use of Japanese expansion if everything made in Japan became the object of hostility? Alarm signals are beginning to be heard in all quarters, not only in America with the exasperation of certain senators, but in Asia too, with the sporadic ceremonial burning of Japanese products.

Surely the good image of the 'Nippon' brand name merits a strategy of greater openness, benevolence, informativeness, and generally improved public relations? All have something to gain by this, Japan as much as anyone. There is an obvious balance between the desirable, the tolerable and the permissible. The balance is to be found in a properly understood reciprocal exchange. That is called economic cooperation, cultural openness and openness of heart, and can be summed up in the formula of co-existence and co-prosperity! These two final words can in fact be found in all the speeches made by Prime Minister Nakasone. And yet, once again, how much is sincerity and how much is strategy? The day when all governments realize that every extreme attitude provokes a similar response, Japanese expansion will be forced either to function with more openness, or to lose face, or to become even more rigid in its approach and precipitate a catastrophe.

Japan is in a hurry to develop as an industrial power, and has never taken the least interest in knowing how others think and react. There is a type of behaviour the Japanese themselves call 'schizophrenic' which is making things very difficult. Economic warfare, Japanese style, presupposes as all wars do a total mobilization of a whole people all the time. But is it possible to keep a whole people in such a state of breathless tension? Whatever their goodwill and their readiness to cooperate, there are already signs, at least in the younger generation, of powerful and open revolt, as many claim their right to live in greater freedom.

The intelligentsia, Japan, and the third way

Today Japan finds herself at the crossroads, caught between the tradition incarnated by the emperor and the democratic example of the West. In between the men in power (politicians and businessmen) and the men of tradition there is the class of intellectuals, or Japanese intelligentsia, a class that is uncertain what position to take up, but which at the very least calls for less conformism and more respect for the individual; an individual respected for himself and not for his membership of, or unconditional subscription to, the collectivity.

The intellectuals are today the only actively critical class in Japan. Nonetheless, only a minority of them exercise an influential role— perhaps 20 of the writers. They are respected because of their fame. The others, including a number of university professors, have only a secondary influence. Their position is extremely difficult, and yet it is vital for the future of Japan. How is it possible to bring liberation, to open people's minds and break open structures, without destroying ancestral unity? And what position should be adopted with regard to the emperor? On the one hand, there is the myth of the emperor who, during the war, incarnated Japanese fascist militarism. On the other hand, without the emperor, Japan would not have arisen so rapidly from the ashes, and the powerful Japan of today would probably not exist.

A few writers among the younger generation, like Asada, denounce the excesses and injustices of the Japanese model. And with justice. Criticism is always necessary; it is the indispensable salt of a society, preventing it from losing its vitality. On the other hand, such writers do not flinch from attacking the emperor himself along with the traditional values of the nation, displaying a lack of understanding in their rejection of what Asada calls the 'broken mandala'. If Japan was really a 'broken mandala', we would be unwise to bank on her surviving. If Japan continues to exist, it is precisely because in spite of everything, she preserves the fundamental virtues of the mandala—symbol of unity, integration, and coherence.

The intelligentsia, the men of culture and knowledge, have a fundamental analytic role to play in researching the delicate balance between transforming and preserving. Their task is to impose openness, synonym of liberty, without falling into the eternal framework of the dualist and formal mind which will go on dominating the West, until the West rediscovers its own traditions and sense of the sacred. The sacred in Japan is not necessarily mystical in the sense in which we understand that word. More than anything else, it is the awareness that each thing and each being possesses an intrinsic value and specificity that command respect. All the subtlety, the sense of harmony, the sense of rapport and of mutual impregnation between one thing and another that characterize art, architecture and Japanese life as a whole arises from this kind of 'sacredness' which we could designate the 'sense of what is', because ultimately all that *is* is worthy of veneration.

Consequently the Japanese example can be extremely inspiring for the West. When the power of money and politics becomes merely a cynical and autocratic force, the intelligentsia has the right of reply. An enlightened and resolute critique is of course neither easy nor very fashionable. To be a man of the present who knows how to integrate the values of the past, one needs a little knowledge, a lot of courage and even more a kind of good sense, if not wisdom. The example of a man like Asada, whose popularity is characteristic of the sickness that is undermining Japan, typifies the intellectuals who destroy their own credibility and undermine the effectiveness of the intelligentsia by the trendy over-simplification of their ideas. Those in power can then easily dismiss the intelligentsia as irresponsible en masse, lumping the good and the bad together: and this allows them to turn the screw a little harder.

The Japan of the young, with their cartoons, their electronic games, their techno-pop music, and their consumerism, needs to be able to breathe. That which is escape today will become questioning tomorrow. And there is a danger that if these young people are not persuaded to get back in line in the name of old traditions, they will lapse into a frenzied modernism, with the attendant risk of a dissolution of all values as in the United States.

If the mandala becomes a symbol of strategy, there is effectively no longer a mandala. If such be the case, Asada is right. But if on the contrary, the mandala is like a tree of life, in which old and new are in harmony, Japan will have a vital role to play for a long time to come. On condition that she really ceases to be what Tadao Umesao described her as, 'a black hole, with everything going in and nothing coming out'.

PART 4

4

HISTORICAL GUIDELINES FOR UNDERSTANDING CONTEMPORARY JAPAN

1. The birth of Japan

Japan the pure and hard has passed through the centuries like a vessel that no storm could sink. Shaped by the apocalyptic hammerblows of modern history, she has risen once more. Where does she get this incomparable force and power that are such a challenge to the western imagination?

Through all the diversity of epochs and situations, Japanese history presents an incomparable continuity. A unity that is at the same time artificial and natural. Artificial because it is a unity that has manifested itself rather late on. Natural because it is a feature of peoples living on relatively small islands separate from a continent.

Primitive Japan was populated by ethnic groups of very different kinds with very little in common. They probably did not even have a common language. The geographical configuration of Japan, made up as it is of very confined valleys sometimes separated by very high mountains, and islands equally separate and with very different climates, has accentuated profound disparities from the beginning.

What was it that brought about their unity, their closeness, what was it that created this feeling of belonging to one and the same land? Where in fact do the Japanese come from?

No one really knows the answer to the last question. They are a mixture of different races, with diverse geographical origins. We do know that the first neolithic civilization (Jomon) may possibly go back to the eighth or fifth millenia BC. Were these first inhabitants of Japan related to the Palaeo-Siberians? Did the first Japanese come from the continent or from the islands of South-East Asia? Archaeologists are still at the stage of hypothesis here.

The first 'warrior' race appeared in the third century AD, having come from Korea. These warrior clans were to have a powerful influence. They were responsible for establishing the houses that were to take power, including the house of Yamato, from which would come the line of the present emperor.

2. Jimmu Tennō, the first mythical emperor

According to the official chronology, Jimmu came to the throne on 11 February 660 BC. Modern historians place the event about four centuries later, around 200 BC. Although the existence of this emperor seems still to belong to the realm of myth, accounts of his life nonetheless evoke the portrait of a living sovereign. In particular, his story symbolizes the warlike long march of the first Japanese towards the East. Starting from Kyūshū, in the South of Japan, this conquest

was to extend as far as the Nara district. After Jimmu Tennō, the accounts in the *Kojiki* and the *Nihon-Shoki*, the two 'bibles' of Shinto tradition, seem more worthy of credence. The fabulous gives way to the historical.

Around the year AD 400, Japan seems to have achieved political unity. The various foreign elements seem to have been assimilated, and an original civilization emerges. It knows of the use of metals, possesses its own religion, and although it does not yet know how to write, it seems ready to accomplish the gigantic leap forward that was to be inspired two centuries later by Chinese culture.

3. The first leap forward

'At the end of the bronze age', write A. Soper, '1,500 years separated Chinese civilization from that of the house of Yamato.' In two centuries, the Japanese were to assimilate the essentials of Chinese culture, leaving the Koreans far behind them. Not until the first shock of the industrial revolution, fourteen centuries later in the Meiji era (1868–1912), would there be another such lightning leap forward. In fact, all through her history, Japan would advance consistently by progressive leaps, leaps that were more and more frequent and more and more remarkable, not to say spectacular.

In the Nara epoch (710–94) the Japanese adopted Chinese culture and institutions, and it is therefore impossible to write the history of Japan without including China, to which Japan owes the essential development of her original culture. In fact it was around the middle of the fifth century that the first signs of writing appeared in Japan, a writing copied from the Chinese *Kanji* (ideograms). In this respect the Japanese had until then been lagging miserably behind existing civilizations, if one considers that Lao Tsu (*Laozi*) and Confucius (*Kongzi*) had already established the bases of Chinese philosophy, that the Phoenicians had invented the alphabet, the Buddha had preached his doctrine nearly twelve centuries earlier . . .

4. The first 'Constitution'

We have to go back as the year 604 to see the first 'governmental act' that would transform Japan (then known as Yamato) at every level, political, religious, and social. The moving spirit behind this Constitution was prince Shōtoku Taishi (who died in 622). I have felt it worth while to publish the whole of this document, for which I am indebted to Louis Frédéric.

1. Respect Wa first of all (*This word means peace, but it also refers to Japan, since Wa was the name by which this country was known to the Chinese. In this first commandment, Shōtoku Taishi or the authors affirm the fundamental national feeling.*) Let your first duty be to avoid discord (*an appeal for national unity*). There are some people who do not love their parents and others who do not obey their masters. These people can cause dissension between themselves and their neighbours. If the upper class lives in harmony with the lower, and if the lower classes follow the best advice, everything will go well, and there will be few insoluble problems. (*Here we see, not the influence of Buddhism, but that of Chinese Confucianism and the recognition of a subordination of social classes, with its concomitant ratification of the existing status quo.*)

2. Venerate with all your heart the three treasures, which are the Buddha, the Dharma (*The Buddhist law*) and the Samgha (*the Buddhist community*), for in these are to be found the ideal life and wisdom of the nation . . . There are not many really bad men. All can be educated (*in Buddhism*). But without the help of these three treasures there can be no hope of straightening out the devious paths of men. (*In this article, Buddhism is officially recommended, and thereby effectively made the State religion.*)

3. Listen reverently to the Imperial Edicts. If the Emperor can be likened to the heavens, his subjects are the earth (*a delicate affirmation of the imperial divinity, a Shinto belief*). With the heaven above and the earth

beneath, unitedly and loyally fulfilling their functions in their respective positions, we shall see the world governed with perfect order and in accord with the harmonious rotation of the four seasons (*a Chinese idea*). If the earth strives to take the place of the heaven, a catastrophe will result. When their lord speaks, let his subjects listen and obey. When he shows the example, they must follow him faithfully. If they disobey, they will do it at their own risk. (*Here Shōtoku Taishi affirms the supremacy of the emperor and his absolute authority.*)

4. All the nobles, whether greater or lesser, must observe the laws (*of the State*) as the roots of all the virtues. In the business of governing the country, the first priority is that of establishing laws. If the upper class does not keep them, the lower classes cannot be governed. If the lower classes do not observe them, they will commit crimes. As long as the law is observed in relationships between the upper and lower classes, a perfect order will prevail and the stability of the State will be assured. (*Here we are aware of a warning to all, nobles and others, intended to ensure governmental authority and maintain the social order.*)

5. When they hear judicial cases concerning ordinary people (*the nobles enjoyed the exclusive privilege of imperial courts*), the judges must 'keep a tight rein on their tongues and hate their own interest'. If there are a thousand cases to judge each day, how many will there be in a year? Hence the necessity for them to show diligence (*to the judges*).

6. Our sages of old taught us to punish the wicked and reward the virtuous. Do not leave anyone's good acts hidden nor any misdeeds unpunished.

7. Each person has a duty to carry out, and must do so with irreproachable diligence. If high positions are given to wise and suitable persons, everyone will approve, but if unworthy workers occupy high positions, that will cause perpetual dissension and strife . . . All the affairs of State, great and small, will be carried out easily provided that good persons hold good positions. This is the basis of a strong State and the lasting prestige of the dynasty. The good leaders of olden times used good men for the top posts and did not give the top posts to their favourites. (*This of course ran counter to the custom of the day according to which important posts were entrusted only to the nobles of certain privileged clans.*)

8. Let all the nobles, greater and lesser, be at their posts from the early morning and go home late. The public affairs to be dealt with are too numerous to allow them to be dealt with by the end of each day.

9 Sincerity is the soul of good conduct. Be sincere at every moment of your life. The success or failure of each job of work you do depends on your sincerity or lack of it. When masters and servants are bound together by feelings of sincerity, there is nothing they cannot do. Every piece of work that is not undertaken in this spirit will come to nothing.

10. Do not give way to anger. Be warm in your forgiveness. Avoid being resentful if others disagree with you. Each one has his own mind and way of thinking. If you are right, I must be wrong. I am not always a saint and you are not always a sinner. We are alike fallible mortals and who is wise enough to judge which of us is good or bad? We are both wise and foolish by turns.

11. Make a distinction between meritorious actions and misdeeds and reward or punish them justly. In our time, merit is not necessarily recompensed and punishments are not always real punishments. Let the nobles, great or small, receive the rewards and punishments they deserve. (*This extends the law to cover those who did not acknowledge its sovereignty over them.*)

12. The governers and masters of the new territories (*those recently conquered by warrior chiefs from aboriginal tribes outside Japan*) must not impose taxes on their peoples. In this country, there are not two sovereigns and the people do not have two masters to serve. There is only one lord, in the person of the emperor. Governors and officers assigned to administer local affairs are themselves also a part of the people and they too are subject to the emperor. (*Here a reaffirmation of imperial authority not only over the people but over local governors who often tended to see themselves as sovereign over their territories and exacted their own separate taxes.*)

13. All governors and officers must share their knowledge about the duties of their office, for their absence owing to illness or travel could cause a temporary interruption in official work.

14. All citizens, whatever their standing, must take care not to be jealous of each other. If you are jealous of others, others will be jealous of you and the vicious circle will be perpetuated.

15. Service of the public at the expense of one's own interest is the duty of a good noble. If a noble's aim is to further his own interest, he provokes the ill-will of the people. If there is such egoism on the one hand and such ill-will on the other, the result will be to the detriment of the public weal. The personal ambition of the shareholders will prevent law and order from reigning. Hence the importance of concord, as was stated in the previous article: it cannot be valued too highly.

16. The sages of old taught us that it is wise to choose the right moment to use the labour of ordinary people for public works. They can be profitably used during the winter months when they have time on their hands. From spring to autumn they are taken up with agricultural and sericultural labours and may not be pressed into service. Without agriculture, how could we all be fed, and without the cultivation of mulberry trees how could we all be clothed?

17. In important affairs, never act alone on the basis of your own judgment, but discuss the matter first with several others. In questions of minor importance, you do not need a great deal of advice.'

These fundamental principles are still those of the Japanese people. such laws were naturally attractive at the time, and they expressed that 'consensus' which still prevails today.

5. The rise of feudal Japan

It is all too often forgotten that modern Japan was born in the Kamakura era (1192–1333), in other words with the emergence of Japanese feudalism. Japanese feudalism apparently came to an end after seven centuries of absolute power with the accession of the emperor Meiji (1868) which marked the end of the military hegemony. In 1870 the emperor formally abolished feudalism and the warrior code known as bushidō. But in spite of all the revolutionary reforms that followed, nothing changed deep down. The aim of those reforms was essentially to give Japan a new structure such as would enable her to face up to Western aggression. How could this be done, except by adopting the military and economic models of the West? It was a decision taken on strategic grounds and in no way represented a conversion of Japan. On the contrary, the more Japan adapted to the West, the more the

Japanese have persisted in remaining apart, preserving themselves intact, and indeed even strengthening their ancient traditional structures. This is the concept of *Wakon-Yōsai*, a popular slogan of the day, meaning 'The Japanese spirit with Western science'. So much so that this twofold current, tradition and modernity, exists as two parallel forces that reinforce one another and contribute more than ever to give Japan a coherence and a power of acting on reality that remain unequalled in the world. In 1869 the emperor created gigantic industrial and commercial consortiums, with the help of former merchants allied to samurai families, such as Mitsubishi, Mitsui and Kinokuniya. To these new men he granted economic monopoly, although he continued to impose the authority of a single central power. The great models for Japan remain precisely those men who succeeded for centuries in maintaining such authority in an iron grip. The first of them was undeniably the earliest shogun of Japan, Minamoto Yoritomo, who in 1185 became the most powerful man in the country after his victory over the rival clan of the Taira. The military government that he proceeded to install from his capital in Kamakura effectively lasted for nearly seven centuries. The other great figures were the shogun Oda Nobunaga (1534–82), Toyotomi Hideyoshi (1536–98) and Tokugawa Ieyasu (1542-1616).

Yoritomo, head of the Minamoto, was one of the greatest Japanese statesmen (1147–99). It was he who set up a private government having an administrative, judiciary and military apparatus. The social, family and even religious life of the Japanese was closely regulated. At this time a symbolic power, that of the emperor, was established alongside the real power. Theoretically the emperor maintained a government and officers at his court. But in reality, what the emperor represented was the spiritual centre of the nation, he was a sacred person and the chief priest of the Shinto religion. And that is still the case today. Throughout Japanese history, the authority of the emperor has never been in question. However, since the time of Yoritomo, the emperor has incarnated much more the spiritual authority and the shogun the administrative office.

Yoritomo, first shogun of Japan, was anxious to establish absolute power. He applied himself to the reduction of the clans, who maintained a certain independence in their remote provinces. He attracted the sympathy of the Buddhist monks by allowing the building of great temples and actively contributing to it. The clergy were protected. The monasteries became refuges of arts and letters. Trade links with China were strengthened. Commerce developed. Yoritomo had realized that he could not establish his power solely on the valour of the samurai and force of arms. The country folk led a life that was often extremely wretched. The peasants had practically no rights, other than the right to work and be endlessly dragooned into forced labour. In their interest he initiated a redistribution of the lands belonging to the aristocrats of Kyōtō. He was deeply attached to the traditional Japan of Shinto, and showed great devotion to Hachiman, his family divinity and kami (or spirit) of war. He showed enormous skill in employing the services of the great feudal landlords with their immense territories, conferring military honours on them when they so deserved, and greatly reinforcing the hierarchy of dependence linking vassals and sovereign. At the same time, all the lords were carefully brought under his supreme jurisdiction, and a special office was set up to keep close watch on the lives of all his vassals. In his view, what mattered was to create a governing class that could bring under one banner all the warriors and at the same time to form coherent classes, (peasants, artisans, serfs), who would all, without exception, be submissive to the central power of the government of the shogunate. Lastly, a rigorous but equitable system of justice, controlled by a special administrative department, and reasonable taxes, set the seal on his power and popularity. For the first time, a truly Japanese spirit appeared. The Japan that had hitherto been divided into 66 provinces now felt itself to be one nation.

6. The defeat of the West: the rejection of Christianity

If Japan is what she is today, she certainly owes it to the Westerners. But the harsh truth is that this is nothing for the West to be proud of. On the contrary. Like any traditional society, Japan was a land that welcomed foreigners, who were *a priori* considered to be honourable and respectable. Thus in 1549, an eminent missionary, father Francis Xavier, was welcomed with great courtesy and honour by the shogun Oda Nobunaga. Xavier was a man of wisdom and high culture, a culture that had been marked by the Jesuits, for whom the precept 'wait and see' is the beginning of all wisdom. Far from imposing his opinions on the Japanese, he strove to understand their customs and the spirit of their country. His Jesuit subtlety, his discretion, his unobtrusive manner even—for he dressed in Japanese costume—worked wonders. The Jesuits have always known how to follow that 'strategy of the unseen' which fitted in so well with the Japanese mentality.

Thus, to begin with things went very well. Christianity took its first steps peaceably under a generally benevolent eye. Francis Xavier was a missionary realist. He appreciated the refinement of Japanese culture, and he understood that a people so strong and so firmly structured could be converted only in prudent stages. In the course of his two years and three months in Japan, he laboured so untiringly that his hair turned white. The important thing, as far as he was concerned, was less to convert a few thousand Japanese in the West of Japan than to find the keys and methods that could be employed by his successors. He appreciated this people for their undeniable openness of mind, their interest in new ideas, their quickness of comprehension, and their capacity to learn well and quickly. His esteem for the Japanese has remained famous through a sentence in a letter he wrote to his colleagues who were evangelizing around Goa, in India: 'Among the non-Christian races, this one is undoubtedly the best.' As a perceptive man, he had noted that the Japanese showed great interest in commercial links with foreign countries. This led him to say in the same letter. 'We must send merchant vessels from Goa, via Malacca, to set up trading posts in the Japanese ports and ask the missionaries to involve themselves in business. That will give us an entrée.' He did not know how apt his words were, for the strategies of the cross, of commerce, and of conquest, clearly amounted to one and the same thing in his mind. To this extent, even for Francis Xavier, the Japanese were in the end only one more part of a whole world of natives he was busily evangelizing.

Then Francis went to the Portuguese colony of Macao, on the coast of China. There he waited for authorization to move into the Great Empire and revive the evangelistic mission work first undertaken there three centuries earlier by Catholic priests under Kubla Khan. The authorization never came. But in Macao he did some hard thinking about the particular conditions required for evangelizing in two such remarkable countries as Japan and China. It was in Macao, too, that he ended his life.

The brothers that Francis Xavier had left in Japan had profited from his finesse and prudence. They managed to make contact with the principal barons in the country and gained appreciable results relatively quickly. By the time Nobunaga died in 1582 the Jesuits had already baptized more than 200,000 disciples and built more than 200 churches, along with a handful of monasteries and numerous schools. At the beginning of the seventeenth century the Company of Jesus had more than doubled this figure. Western infleunce began to make itself gently felt on the traditional structure of Japan. If the Jesuits had had the monopoly of evangelistic activity, it is probable that Christian expansion would have reached the proportions of the sixth century Buddhist conquest.

Nonetheless, the Jesuits were not above reproach. There was a tendency among them to believe that the supremacy of the cross should obliterate all other authority, including that of the emperor. Hideyoshi, successor to Nobunaga, was benevolent towards the Christian missionaries, but he became aware of the danger and abruptly promulgated edicts commanding the Jesuits to leave the country in 20 days. However, he changed his mind and did not enforce this decree.

The Westerners ought to have sensed the change of mood and taken even greater care to adopt a low profile. But the Spanish who had settled in the Phillipines were jealous of the successes of the Jesuits under Portuguese protection. They sent Franciscan brothers who openly propagandized against the two fundamental religions of Japan, Shinto and Buddhism. Until then the apparent submissiveness of the Christians vis-à-vis the central power had been reassuring, but Hideyoshi was extremely annoyed by this competition between the Spanish and Portugese missionaries. Christian barons began to fight among themselves and there were various disturbances in the South of the country. By the time he died, Hideyoshi had become resolutely opposed to Christianity.

The first serious persecution of Christians was triggered off by an event that was both extraordinarily gratuitous and revealing. A Spanish vessel, the *San Felipe*, was damaged as a result of a typhoon, and became the object of a rather curious act of piracy on the part of the Japanese. The Japanese pilot who was supposed to be guiding it towards the place for repairing ships managed to wreck the boat and break its back. Whereupon the Japanese set-to and pillaged the boat, on the basis of an ancient Japanese law according to which any wrecked ship becomes the property of the person who discovers it. When Hideyoshi was told about this he expressed approval for the behaviour of his subjects.

The Spanish pilot of the *San Felipe* was furious and tried to intimidate the Japanese by showing them on a map all the Spanish possessions in the world and announcing how dangerous it was to offend a sovereign so powerful as Philip II. 'How has Spain acquired so many territories?' asked the Japanese. The pilot then gave a reply that was as naïve as it was dangerous: 'First of all they send priests to the countries they intend to conquer. When there are enough conversions the traders arrive and after them come the soldiers who proceed to conquer the country.'

This conversation was immediately reported via a special courier to Hideyoshi, and he flew into a violent rage. It was a confirmation of his worst fears. He gave immediate orders that the Franciscans in Osaka and a few Jesuits be crucified at once, though as an act of mercy they were to be speared twice first. He drew up an edict with five articles, dated 24 July 1587, that proscribed the Christian religion as contrary to the traditional religions of Japan, Shinto and Buddhism. One hundred and thirty-seven churches in the neighbourhood of Nagasaki were destroyed and all the Jesuits were rounded up to be deported. A short time after these edicts, Hideyoshi died. His successor, Tokugawa Ieyasu (1542–1616), had a more conciliatory outlook, and suspended the execution of these measures.

The Jesuit fathers hastily returned, and manifested their inability to comprehend the Japanese mind by the readiness with which they took up their proselytizing and intriguing all over again. In 1600 a Dutch vessel came to Japan. The Spanish Jesuits feared this competition and denounced the newcomers as pirates. This strategem came to the attention of the shogun Ieyasu, who happily granted an audience to the pilot of the vessel, a remarkable English sailor named Will Adams. It was a historic interview. Will Adams gave him some excellent advice and not only obtained permission to remain in Japan but was even accorded the highest consultative position ever accorded to a white man. He gave an objective description of the squabbles in the Christian world and the contempt felt by most Europeans for the brutal methods of conquest employed by the Spanish and Portuguese. Ieyasu was determined to discover whether Adams' assertions were true and sent a Japanese scholar, Nishi Sōshin, to Europe. This man was received at the royal courts and by the cardinals with all the appropriate honours, but in Spain he was able to witness the horrors of the Inquisition of Torquemada at first hand.

A few years later his report was confirmed by that of a Japanese priest, Araki, in whose presence courtiers and Jesuits talked quite openly of their desire to conquer Japan. Araki felt insulted by the fact that they could think him capable of denying his own country and returned to Japan to warn the shogun against his fellow-Christians. In 1611 the shogun banished all the Christians from his court: three years later, all the priests, Japanese and European, were unceremoniously deported to Macao, the churches were demolished and the congregations scattered and put under a ban. When the shogun died, his successor, Tokugawa Iemitsu, forbade Japanese Christians to travel abroad or engage in trade. All relations with the Spanish were broken off. Japan was progressively closing to all foreign influence. Between 1633 and 1639 several decrees confirmed this isolation. No Japanese could henceforth leave the shores of the islands, and every man, woman and child in the country had to go to the Buddhist or Shinto sanctuaries and obtain certificates attesting that they were not Christians. In 1637 the Christian community at Shimabara in the South rose in revolt. Thirty to forty thousand Christian samurai and peasants withstood the troops of the shogun, until the Christian Dutch, who were desperate to curry favour with the Japanese, took it into their heads to bombard the fortifications from their vessels. Thirty-seven thousand persons perished in the ensuing massacre, terminated by the shogun's troops.

The net result was that the Japanese despised the Dutch all the more, distrusting such faithless and lawless men, and confined them to the tiny island of Deshima at Nagasaki within high palisades, while limiting their trade to two ships a year. The enclave of Nagasaki was carefully preserved from external influence and remained the sole trading-post between Japan and the outer world. After 1635 Japan thus remained, for all practical purposes, in a state of isolation until the nineteenth century, in other words for two and a half centuries.

Their only contacts with the rest of the world were two Dutch boats and ten Chinese junks a year. In 1640 a Portugese mission attempted to break through the isolation. All except 13 were put to death, and the survivors came back with the following order: 'In future let no one sail towards Japan, not even as an ambassador, as long as the sun shines on the earth. This declaration will never be revoked, it will be maintained on pain of death.'

No other nation throughout history has been capable of such a power of self-sufficiency. For Japan this was her longest period of peace. The feudal structure of the country was strengthened and the importance of Japan on the international scene diminished. True, not everything was rosy, and a few famines could have been avoided by recourse to normal trade exchanges. But on the whole the advantages of peace outweighed these disadvantages. Japanese art and culture bloomed, and everyone could live in serenity. Japan became the land of the gods once more.

7. Dictatorship and unity

Around 1573 there emerged three 'great captains' who were to become the three greatest dictator generals Japan has ever seen: Oda Nobunaga (1534–82), Toyotomi Hideyoshi (1536–98) and Tokugawa Ieyasu (1542–1616).

Paradoxically, all three were of modest birth, although up till then all the great men of Japan had come from the class of the aristocracy. With these three, Japan was for a time to experience a new era, stretching over 24 or 25 years. These were the men who were to lay the solid foundation for the social, political and economic unity of Japan.

All the clans that hitherto had been warring among themselves were to be conquered in turn by Oda Nobunaga, then by his successors. They were forced to submit and obey the central power. One small point should be noted: the army of Oda Nobunaga was made up, not of the traditional samurai, but of soldiers of fortune, many of whom were formerly brigands. He imposed a very harsh discipline on them, while exploiting their cunningness, their adaptability and their general mobility. Nobunaga's strategic intelligence did the rest. Despite the smallness of his army, he succeeded in crushing enemies whose troops were far more numerous. In order to defend his land, he had to fight a powerful baron, Imagawa. He drew the latter's army into the gorges of Okeharama, which he knew like the back of his hand, and totally destroyed it. Imagawa himself was killed in the course of this battle. Fortified by this initial success, Nobunaga's army attacked other fiefs one after the other. In the meantime, the size of the territories he had taken by conquest kept on growing. On 15 November 1568 he siezed Kyōto. Such was the discipline of his troops—who did not pillage the town—and such was the order that Nobunaga imposed there, that the population was won round to his side, as were some of the leading families close to the imperial circle.

One by one the *daimyō* of ten provinces came to offer him their allegiance. After each of his victories, Nobunaga would make a generous distribution of his lands among his warriors, thus reinforcing their fidelity. Superbly backed up by his generals Ieyasu and Hideyoshi, Nobunaga destroyed the warrior-monks of Enryakuji and burnt the monasteries of Mount Hiei, thereby managing to destroy priceless works of art. But during a stay in Kyōto, he was betrayed by one of his generals, Akechi, who attacked him with his troops, killing his eldest son. However, Hideyoshi fought back against Akechi, defeating and killing him.

8. Hideyoshi and the unification of Japan

Even though he could not read, Toyotomi Hideyoshi remains one of the great figures in Japanese history. He showed himself as good a strategist as he was an administrator. He was the first to order a census and to fix a tax that all had to pay. In order to establish his authority, Hideyoshi was to fix the form of Japanese society with draconian thoroughness.

He had a census made of all the territories in Japan, and forbade the peasants to possess arms or to leave their lands under penalty of sanctions that went far beyond the death of the guilty: 'If a peasant abandons his fields, either to become a trader or to hire out his labour, not only must he be punished, but his whole village must be put on trial with him. All those who are neither employed on military service nor in agriculture must be sought out by the local authorities and expelled . . . Where peasants engaging in trade have been kept concealed, the whole village or town will be held responsible for this infringement of the law.'

Henceforth the lot of the peasant would be the life of a serf: he would be immobilized, pressurized, terrified by the idea of the misdeeds that others might commit and for which he would have to pay the penalty, at the mercy of informers, more miserable than ever, condemned to forced labour so as not to die of hunger. He was liberated from his servitude only at the end of the nineteenth century.

This principle of collective responsibility has been the rule in Japan for centuries. A peasant who showed the least sign of rebellion could be put to death together with his whole family. If necessary, the village itself could be razed and all its inhabitants annihilated. As a general rule, soldiers and peasants were divided into groups of five or ten persons who acted in solidarity with one another. A samurai who left his master without permission could not be taken on by any other lord. As to the barons themselves, their condition, all things considered, was no more enviable.

Oda Nobunaga, Hideyoshi and Ieyasu, the three Japanese dictators who followed one another, knew perfectly well how to dominate the *daimyō*. All the actions of the latter were subjected to tyrannical rules. They could not absent themselves from the court at Kyōto without leaving their families hostage, and they were limited to retinues of 20 armed men. Financially pressured, ruthlessly reduced by the power of an absolute despotism, the Japanese of all social classes could not do otherwise than resign themselves. Moreover, there was an espionage system by which the shogun kept the country under a surveillance that was both visible and invisible.

9. The subjection of Korea and the invasion of China

Hideyoshi's great dream was to sieze Korea and reign over China. In 1592 he invaded Korea at the head of an army 200,000 strong. Initially, the Korean armies were easily defeated, but with the help of the Chinese, the Koreans got a grip on the situation and managed to retake Seoul in 1593. The advance of the Japanese armies was blocked. Furthermore, the Korean fleet under Admiral Yi destroyed numerous Japanese vessels. The Koreans were superior tactically and strategically at sea, and they also possessed terrible 'tortoise ships', forerunners of our armoured boats, which were covered with armour plating and equipped with rams that cut through other boats when they struck them.

Hideyoshi found himself obliged to negotiate, and made some surprising proposals: he asked for the re-establishment of trade relations between China and Japan, broken off since 1548: and he also asked for a daughter of the emperor of China to be sent to become the wife of the emperor of Japan.

Hideyoshi did not succeed in invading China. Moreover, in his old age it seems that he was close to madness. In September 1598, at the age of 63, he succumbed to illness in his Palace at Fushimi.

10. The end of isolationism

The opening of feudal Japan to the West cost the people 50 years of heroic sacrificial striving. It is a prodigious saga that has never really been told. When Admiral Perry arrived with his boats, and his troops were able to parade with complete impunity, the Japanese endured a frightful trauma. What the Mongols had failed twice to achieve, the conquest of Japan, seemed likely to become a reality, and the new barbarians, buoyed up with their firearms and their technological superiority, threatened to become the first conquerors. The Japanese understood right away that the policy of blind protectionism no longer had any purpose. The extent of their volte-face was a measure of their stupefaction.

Astounded and petrified, the Japanese suddenly became aware that an unknown civilization, with access to considerable technical and military resources, could bring Japan to her knees. This was unthinkable for them, since their national territory had always been nothing less than the land of the gods, of the kami, and therefore sacred. Out of this profound trauma was born modern Japan.

The Japanese would adapt to modern times with unprecedented speed. The anachronistic nature of feudalism was at once apparent. The shogun, or prime minister, who governed in place of the emperor, handed power back to the latter in 1868. The floodgates to reform had been opened.

On 8 July 1853, four American vessels, 'black boats' commanded by Commodore Perry, arrived at Edo (Tokyo). They brought a message from the President of the United States to 'His Imperial Majesty the Emperor of Japan': the President required only the freedom for American boats to enter a Southern Japanese port for the purpose of revictualling. This event placed the Japanese government in a position of considerable embarrassment. It seemed unthinkable that Japan should be opened up to foreigners. Perry announced that he would be back for the reply *in a year*. He was faithful to his promise. In the meantime, the Japanese had thought long and hard over what policy to adopt.

The fact was that after such a lengthy period of isolation, Japan was simply not in a position to resist foreigners. If it came to war, there was a real danger that the military superiority of the westerners would prove decisive. On 31 March 1854 a 'treaty of peace and friendship' was signed between the USA and the Empire of Japan. As far as the Japanese were concerned, this option represented a way of temporizing while struggling to put together as quickly as possible an army and a fleet strong enough to withstand the westerners.

On 7 December 1857, Townsend Harris, the first minister plenipotentiary of the US in Japan, was finally granted a solemn audience with the shogun Iesada. One scene from this visit is sufficient to convey what could be the nature of such a meeting between two men of whom one symbolized the new Western world, the other the Cult of Ancestors. When Townsend Harris eventually came before the shogun, the face of this all-powerful man was hidden by a curtain hung from the ceiling. Ultimately obliged to receive this 'barbarian', the representative of the ancestors was there all right, but as an invisible presence. Now, as then, we continue to question the meaning of that hidden face.

In 1870 the Emperor Meiji formally abolished feudalism; at the same time, the famous samurai lost all their prerogatives and even found themselves prohibited from wearing their swords (1875). They were obliged to abandon their traditional hairstyle, which had involved having the front part of the head completely shaved, and the hair on the back part gathered up on the nape and tied on the top of the head.

Overnight, the samurai, who had up till then formed the first class in Japan (apart from the courtiers and nobles), saw their very existence denied and their knowledge declared useless.

The majority of the 400,000 to 500,000 samurai of the day in Japan were prepared to toe the line; they agreed to take command of a 'mob' from classes previously considered inferior: peasants, merchants or artisans. Certain of the samurai actually sent their daughters (and even occasionally their sons) to work in factories.

Saigō Takamori and 40,000 other samurai preferred to die; they opted to throw themselves into the final battle, the battle of despair, for the sake of their honour. Voluntarily armed only with their own swords, they courageously faced the imperial troops with their rifles, and only a tiny minority escaped from what amounted to a thinly-disguised form of collective suicide. Saigō Takamori was wounded in the battle, and made one of his friends cut off his head. With him disappeared one of the last great samurai.

From this time on, the samurai were split into two camps; those who wished to remain faithful to the traditional teaching of their school, or *ryū*, and who for the most part took refuge in the country: they took up other vocations but continued to practise their training nonetheless. The others became integrated into the life of modern Japan, and contributed in a leadership role to the rise of the new nation. Some chose to adapt their previously secret knowledge of fighting for a wider public: thus were born jūdō, karate, and aikidō.

11. Japanese militarism and Great Japan (1937-45)

After the revolt of Saigō Takamori had been crushed in 1877, there appeared a strange man, Tōyama Mitsuru, aged 23. Tōyama wanted a country that was pure and hard. He dreamed of a Japan faithful to her origins, to the kami, faithful to the veneration of the emperor. He rejected an imperial regime that was becoming constitutional. A conspirator as much as he was an ascetic, Tōyama Mitsuru wanted to avenge the death of Saigō Takamori. Not long afterwards, Okubo Toshimichi, the Minister of the Interior, was assassinated. From now on, the 'pure Nipponese spirit' must reign alone. The military clans took power. On 1 August 1894, Japan declared war on China. A lightning war brought the victorious Japanese to the gates of Peking. They landed in Korea, took Port Arthur, and entered Manchuria. But the Japanese had to give up Port Arthur, which was to be occupied by the Russians. Tōyama Mitsuru then became the moving spirit in a gigantic secret society, 'the Black Dragon', which spread its tentacles from Turkestan to Manchuria. Members swore to eject Europeans from the oriental world. In a few years, numerous moderate personalities were assassinated one by one. The authors of these so-called 'patriotic' crimes were greatly admired. The tribunals inflicted only nominal penalties. The conspirators thus managed to liquidate all the important members of the government and submitted their demands to His Imperial Majesty:

— That criminal counsellors be removed
— That all political parties be dissolved
— Lastly, that the ultranationalist general Araki Sadao should be named Commander in Chief of the army of Manchuria.

The greatest rebellion in modern Japanese history ended tragically. The emperor rejected the demands of the mutineers and they were all executed.

After this the military-nationalist representatives of the coalition occupied the key posts in the State. Once the military were established in a dictatorial position, they felt ready to take on the world. They feared neither the immensity of China nor the US. They spent eight years (1937–45) trying to draw every Japanese into the myth of Great Japan.

Dai Nihon, 'Great Japan', was the period when the nationalist leadership believed in Japanese domination over the whole of eastern Asia and Oceania.

Japan 1945

However, at the beginning of 1945, Japan found herself in a very grave situation. The defensive perimeter of the Pacific had given way, the blockade and the bombardments were irrefutable proof that the enemy was drawing closer to the metropolitan territory. In spite of the exhaustion of the population and the scepticism of certain politicians, the military men still carried on proclaiming their faith in ultimate victory, and through the summer of 1945 they were making feverish preparations for the defence of the national sanctuary, planning a desperate effort to crush the enemy the moment he set foot on the soil of the fatherland.

The exploding of the two atomic bombs on 6 and 9 August of 1945 over Hiroshima and Nagasaki, with the simultaneous entry of Russia on the scene in the shape of an invasion of Manchuria, created an extraordinary fever in the Japanese cabinet. Endless debates took place to decide whether or not the war should be continued. Ultimately, the only question that really remained concerned the safeguard and protection of the imperial institutions.

The peace party eventually won the day. It was agreed that a rapid end to hostilities was precisely the surest means to preserve the imperial institutions.

For the first time in the history of Japan, the emperor himself—Hirohito—addressed the nation. On 15 August 1945, he read a message on the radio couched in terms that were however so archaic and contorted that most of the country took several hours to comprehend that the emperor had agreed to unconditional surrender.

Ultimately, it was just this unconditional solidarity of Japan with her emperor that once again saved the country from dismemberment. The US was obliged to recognize in the emperor the only spokesman who could reconstruct a Japan that would be different from the one that had collapsed.

GLOSSARY

Ai
Love, harmony, unification.

Aikidō
'The way of harmony with universal energy.' A martial art developed in Japan in 1931 by master Morihei Ueshiba.

The techniques of aikidō are divided into two categories: *the nagewaza*, throwing techniques, and the *katame-waza*, control techniques. The founding of the *Aikikai aikidō* association dates from 9 February 1948.

Aiki-jutsu
A fighting technique, forerunner of *aikidō*.

Amaterasu-Ōmi Kami: 'The great and august divinity who shines in heaven.'
Goddess of the Sun in *Shinto*, Amaterasu is the daughter of the primordial couple Izanagi-Izanami and great-great grandmother of Jimmu, first mythical emperor of Japan.

Bodhidharma or Daruma in Japanese.
The first patriarch of Zen (*chan* in China) (460–534), twenty-eighth patriarch after the Buddha. According to tradition, he went from India to Southern China in the sixth century and later settled at the temple of Shao Lin (Shōrin), where he trained monks in a form of unarmed combat in order to toughen them in mind and body. However, his life remains legendary for the most part.

Bo-jutsu
Techniques for fighting with a long stick. *Bo-jutsu* is studied in a complementary way in the *karate*, *kendō*, and *aikidō dōjō's*. Japanese technique has developed from the Chinese and involves sliding the

stick through the hands somewhat like in billiards.

Bokuseki (or calligraphy)
Calligraphy is a major Japanese art-form. Often practised in connection with the tea ceremony. Specimens of ancient calligraphy from the work of grand masters are priceless treasures in Japan.

Budō
Japanese martial arts. *Budō* (from *bu*, warrior, and *dō*, the way) signifies the way of the warrior, self-defence.

Budō is to be distinguished from *bu-jutsu* (from *bu*, warrior, and *jutsu*, technique) because *budō* belongs to the spiritual level (the current of the divine heart) and *jutsu* to the physical level (strength, intelligence).

Bu also signifies the way of harmony and reconciliation. The Chinese or Japanese character 'Bu' means 'halting of the sword'.

Bushi
Japanese warrior of the feudal era, samurai. The virtues of the *bushi* are:
— *Dōryo*: magnanimity.
— *Shiki*: resolution.
— *Onsha*: generosity, tolerance.
— *Fudō*: posture and attitude, immovability.
— *Giri*: duty.
— *Ninyo*: magnanimity (on a different level from *dōryo*).

Bushidō
'The code of the warrior.' Code of honour of the Japanese warrior. The word was popularized by Inazo Nitobe, in his work '*Bushidō, the soul of Japan*', published at the beginning of the century, and it defines the code of honouring the ancestors: a spiritual law that Japanese nationalists are particularly keen to exalt. Rectitude, justice, courage, contempt for death, benevolence, politeness, sincerity, honour, loyalty and self-mastery are the principal rules of Bushidō.

Ch'an (Chan)
A Chinese Buddhist type of philosophical thought that evolved from the Indian *dhyāna*: Introduced to Japan where it was known as Zen.

Chanoyu
Tea ceremony. Familiar term for 'sa-dō', way of tea.

Ch'i
Chinese word for vital energy, equivalent of Japanese *ki* or Hindu *prāna* (also written *qi*).

Dō
Way, spiritual path. Signifies both way and goal. The goal is also the way. See also *michi* and *tao*.

Dōgen
Founder of the Sōtō sect in *Zen*, after his study trip to China.

Dōjō
Martial arts school, training hall. *Dō* signifies 'the way', *jō* the 'place'.

Fudōshin
Imperturbable and calm spirit in the face of danger.

Fuji (mount)
Mountains are sacred in Japan, especially Mount Fuji, which is the most sacred mountain in the country. Every year, thousands of people climb Fuji. Many of them are dressed in white, symbol of purity. The name originates in the Ainu language, 'mountain of fire'.

Funakoshi Gishin
Founder of modern *karate*, around 1921.

Geidō
Artistic or artisanal way. *Gei*: art.

Genshin
Power to parry or anticipate an attack, kind of intuition or premonition.

Gokin
Secrets that are revealed only to the disciples who reach the final stage of the journey.

Hashi
Signifies 'binding two things on the top'. In relation to space-time it is thus defined by its extremities. Each thing that has an end thereby creates another. Crossing, filling, extending in space are expressed by *hashi*. Every hierarchy is also *hashi*.

Hachiman
God of war. Minamoto Yoritomo, for whom he was the protecting divinity, built him a very fine sanctuary at Kamakura. There are thousands of these in Japan.

Hagakure
Means 'hidden under the leaves', the title of a famous work on *Bushidō*

in 11 volumes completed in 1716, by Yamamoto Tsunetomo.

Hakama
Skirt-trouser worn for *kendō*, *kyūdō*, and *aikidō*; also still a part of Japanese traditional ceremonial dress for Japanese women.

Hanshi
Higher teacher. It is possible to be a *hanshi* from the eighth dan onwards. *Shihan* signifies grand master. But the Grand Master must also be a *hanshi* and at least ninth dan. Thus the hierarchy is: renshi, kyōshi, hanshi, shihan.

Hara
Stomach. Centre. The *hara* designates the area of the lower stomach, situated below the navel. For the Japanese this area is the original centre of man, the centre of psychic gravity where the deep vital forces are concentrated. It is through the *hara* that a man communicates with the primordial unity of all things. See also *tanden*.

Hiden
Secret tradition, arcanum, hidden knowledge.

Himorogi
A sacred place visited by the *kami* or spirits. This space is defined by four posts joined by a cord and on which are placed little pieces of paper (*gohei*).

Hontai
Expresses the mastery of the body by the mind.

Iai-jutsu
The art of drawing the sword. Solitary training based on speed and concentration.

Irimi
A term employed particularly in *aikidō*. Expresses the art of non-resistance, consisting in allowing the adversary's force, however great, to turn against itself (see *tenkan*).

Ikebana
'Placing living flowers in water.' Floral art implying the duty of loving flowers for themselves. A Japanese bows before the flower arrangement that he has executed himself.

Jū
Suppleness.

Jūdō

Martial art founded by Jigorō Kanō (1860–1938): its ancestor is *Jū-jutsu*. The term *jūdō* was already in use, before Kanō, by the school of Jikishin-Ryū, but it was Kanō who expounded and popularized its fundamental principle.

Jū-jutsu

Techniques for unarmed combat based on the principles of non-resistance, ancestor of *jūdō* (from *Jū*: supple, yield, obey, weak, gentle, peaceful, and *jutsu*: technique, science).

Jū-jutsu signifies an art or practice of suppleness which consists in giving way initially in order to win in the end.

Junshi

Custom of following one's master in death; also, collective suicide.

Kadō

The way of flowers. See also *Ikebana*.

Kami

Shinto word to designate deities. The *kami* are numberless. A man, a waterfall, a tree, a rock may be *kami*. Fulfilling one's form harmoniously, taking on one's destiny while giving evidence of unmistakable virtues are, among others, conditions for acquiring the quality of *kami*. Every *kami* is worthy of veneration.

Kamidana

Shinto family altar, cult of ancestors (as opposed to *butsudana*, or Buddhist family altar).

Kamikaze

'Divine wind': name of the typhoon that devastated the Mongol fleet in 1280, given by analogy to suicide pilots during the last war.

Kangeikō

Special winter training in all the martial arts. For eight to ten days, training is pushed to the limits of physical resistance. A similar training during the hottest days of summer is called *Shōchū geikō*.

Kanō, Jigorō,

Founder of *jūdō* (1860–1938), creator of the *Kōdō-Kan* school.

Kappō

Art of resuscitating through the *Kuatsu* (or technique of reanimation through the *kiai*).

Kata

Combat patterns according to established rules. Series of blows aimed at imaginary opponents.

Katana

One-edged sword, worn slipped into the belt, *tachi* if worn hung from the belt. It is categorized in three principal groups according to length: less than 30cm, *tantō* (dagger); from 30 to 61cm *shōtō* (short sword); more than 61cm, *daitō* (long sword). A pair of long and short swords is called *daishō*.

Keīko

Training, in a general sense. *Kei*: go beyond, surpass; Kō, ancestors, ancient. *Keidō*: also becoming aware of the totality of the past.

Kendō

To begin with, the art of the sword. All the rules of the sword are applicable to *kendō*. However, combat is actually engaged with a weapon known as *shinai*, made out of four strips of bamboo bound together. The equipment is: *men* (mask), *dō* (breastplate), *kote*(guard for the wrist and forearm).

Kenpō (or Kempō)

Way of the fist. Martial art of Chinese origin. Around 1600, Chinese military men settled in Okinawa and taught the islanders *kenpō*. The latter combined *kenpō* with their own method, and there resulted a new form of combat called *Okinawa-te*, the real forerunner of *karate*.

Kensho

'Seeing within one's own nature: semantically, *kensho* and *satori* have practically the same meaning and the two terms are used interchangeably. To speak of the enlightenment of the Buddha and the patriarchs, *satori* is more commonly used, as implying a deeper experience. The most exact Japanese formula for defining total illumination is *daigo tettei*.

Kenjutsu

Art of the sword, forerunner of *kendō*.

Ki

Energy. The manifestation of the vital inner energy that is to be found in every man, and which is none other than the original creative energy of the earth and the Universe.

In Japanese, the word *ki* signifies both breath and attention. *Ki* is thus the fundamental energy of being, beyond physical, chemical or natural phenomena. Attention, mental force is itself *ki*, and therefore it can be directed into every part of the body or turned outwards towards the external world. It is customary to speak of *ki* as being concentrated in the abdomen (*seika-tanden*).

The word *ki* is in the Japanese language formed from the signs that represent the word rice. The word rice is itself formed from ideogrammes representing water and fire. In other words, the cosmic energy symbolized by water and fire is concentrated in its manifestation so as to create the energy of *ki*, which is none other than the original energy.

Kiai

Concentration of *ki*, shout. The opposite of *aiki*. The shout is an expression of energy.

Kihon

The technique of basic movements in all the *budō*.

Kōan

In *Zen* Buddhism, a *kōan* is an enigma, a paradox, a seemingly absurd question or problem that cannot be resolved by way of the intellect. Example:
'What is the nature of the Buddha?'
'It is the tree at the bottom of the garden.'
Or the *kōan* of the Zen monk Hakuin Ekaku:
'What sound is produced by the clapping of a single hand?' The *kōan* serves to go beyond discursive intelligence; once understood, it provokes an awakening in the depths of the mind.

Ko-budō

An ancient martial art (from *ko*: ancient and *budō*: martial art). It is also supplied to the minor martial arts.

Kokoro

Heart, will, intention, mind, idea, thought. Absolute reality is *Kokoro* (with a capital K).

Kokū

A unit for weighing rice (180 litres) with which the samurai were paid.

Kokutai

Expresses the awareness of Japan's unity and sacred nature.

Kokyū

Breathing, movement of psychical force or *ki*, or else movement of the body in accordance with *ki*. A strong *kokyū* indicates a body endowed with *ki*, or intense psychic and spiritual energy. The Universe itself is the functioning of *Kokyū*. *Kokyū hō* is the way of leading others thanks to *kokyū*, *kokyū nage* is the art of throwing others with the aid of *Kokyū*. *Fukushiki kokyū* is deep abdominal breathing.

Ko-Shintō

The ancient original Shinto.

Kung-Fu (or Gongfu)

'Human effort', a fist technique, generic name for Chinese martial arts, *kenpō*.

Kurai

A peaceful mental state (like an object floating on the water). Expresses the idea of a state that offers no resistance. In combat, its means adapting to the will of one's adversary until the latter relaxes his effort, the right moment to react.

Kyūba no michi

'The way of the bow and the horse' was the first, originally orally transmitted, code of the samurai at the end of the twelfth century.

Kyūdō

The way of the bow.

Kyū-jutsu

The technique of the bow.

Kyūsho

The vital points of the enemy.

Lao-tsu (or Laozi)

Although Lao-Tsu is generally considered to be one of the greatest Chinese teachers, little is known about his life. It is said that he was born about 604 BC and that he drew up the 'bible' of Taoism, the *Tao-te-Ching*. The Tao has been defined as 'the foundation of all existence', 'the power of the universe' or 'the Way'.

Ma

Space and time. It designates a natural and uninterrupted interval between two things.

A space limited by pillars and a screen is also *ma*. The art of *ma* impregnates the whole of Japanese culture (architecture, painting,

music, theatre, etc.).
Space and time are not separate. They arise from one single concept. Each thing derives its integrity and definiteness from its space-time.

Ma-ai
Indicates the distance between oneself and one's adversary. The science of *ma-ai* consists in sensing the right distance to establish harmony with a partner.
To penetrate the *ma-ai* of the partner is to have won the victory over him in advance.

Makimono
A scroll, in the sense of a diploma.

Matsuri
Festival. These festivals are both sacred and popular and there are very many of them in Japan. They provide an opportunity to venerate the *kami* (or spirits). Chiefly Shinto but also Buddhist, the *matsuri* all involve processions and popular dances. The *matsuri* serve to invoke the souls of the ancestors or deceased parents before the family altar (*kami-dana*) and also to create an enormous popular parade with lines of floats that are often sumptuously decorated (as with the festivals of *Gion* at Kyōto. Each temple and each village has its *matsuri*).

Misogi-harai
Expresses a process of spiritual, moral and physical decontamination and purification.

Mu
Nothing, vacuity. *Zen* concept. In *Zen*: identification of the one and the whole.

Muga-mushin
Annihilation of one's self and one's mind.
Mushin, the non-mental, is to be distinguished from *Yushin*, the present mental, that is to say the mental that fixes on a point and becomes 'superficial'.

Munen Mushin (or Munen muso)
State without idea and without thought.

Mondo
Term in Japanese *Zen* signifying a form of rapid dialogue between master and pupil. The practice of *mondo* is utilized to go beyond the conventional procedures of conceptual thought.

Mushashūgyō
'The roaming of the warrior.' Going from school to school, from *dōjō* to *dōjō*, to develop one's knowledge and meet new partners.

O-bon
Festival of the dead on 13 and 14 July. The dead are closely associated with the living. As homage to the dead, there is dancing of traditional dances, or concerts by orchestras of *taiko*, enormous drums that are beaten with great force.

Rinzai-shū
One of the Japanese Zen sects, from the name of its founder (in Chinese: Lin Zi).

Rōnin
Samurai without work, through the disgrace or death of his master.

Rōshi
Title of a monk who is advanced in *Zen*.

Ryū
Martial arts school.

Sabi
Expresses a taste, a subtle flavour, a sensibility. In the realm of poetry, *sabi* denotes the world of vision; a very pure sensibility.

Sakura
Cherry tree. The *sakura* flower symbolizes ephemeral beauty, the disinterested love of life. It expresses the idea of dying, in the sense of detaching oneself completely from life, as the flower of the cherry tree detaches itself spontaneously from the tree.

Samu
Concentration on manual work.

Samurai
Japanese warrior having the right to wear two swords. Upper class in Japanese society. The other classes are, in order, peasants, artisans and merchants (leaving aside the aristocracy and those dedicated to religion).

Satori
Zen term denoting spiritual illumination or awakening.
Satori is essentially an experience, a sudden realization. An indefinable experience that conveys sudden illumination, an intuitive and profound comprehension of a hidden reality.

Sen

Initiative (analyzing the situation in which the adversary finds himself). *Gono-sen*, when one is attacked, expresses the idea of blocking and counter-attacking. *Sen-no-sen*, the idea of attacking before the adversary's attack has begun.

Sen-no-Rikyū

(1521–1571). Known as the greatest master of the tea ceremony (*cha-no-yu*). The rules of his school (*senke*) are still applied today. The tea ceremony is of Zen inspiration and also expresses the spirit of *Wabi* (**q.v.**) or simplicity.

Sensei

Signifies teacher or master. A word used to express one's respect or admiration. A little hackneyed nowadays.

Seppuku

An elegant term for *hara-kiri*, or the act of killing oneself by self-disembowelling with a short sword; a privilege reserved for the samurai in the feudal era.

Sesshin

Rigorous spiritual discipline, concentration of thought. Used particularly in Zen.

Setsubun

February festival. The evil spirits are ejected through the throwing of beans on the first day of Spring into the nooks and crannies of the house.

Shadō

Way of archery. See also kyūdo.

Shiai

Competition, test.

Shime-nawa

A rope surrounding places or all things venerated in Shinto.

Shin

Heart, mind, character. It is in the heart that the Japanese situate the soul, the intellect, all that provokes or evokes a feeling, a moral force. (See also *Kokoro*.)

Shingitai

In martial arts, signifies the three qualities of the particular grade (dan): *shin* (spirit, character), *gi* (technique in the art practised), *tai* (corporal elements). Or *shin* (heavens), *gi*, (earth), *tai*, (man); reuniting the three elements.

Shinpan
Judge, referee.

Shinai
Bamboo sword used in *kendō*.

Shinobu-koi
A love that is hidden and secret.

Shintō
Word expressing the original religion of Japan and signifying 'the way of the gods'. The word *Shinto* was not defined until 560 AD to distinguish old Japanese religious practices — until then expressed only as the *way*—from the growing influence of Japanese Buddhism. Expresses the rhythm of life and nature.

Shōdo
Art of writing, of calligraphy.

Shōgun
Name given to the military governor of Japan prior to the Meiji era. The *shōgun* was always invested by the emperor, his office was often hereditary. The *shōgun* held the real power for centuries. Original meaning: 'general against the barbarians'.

Sōgyo
Heavens. *Sō*, man; *gyō*, Earth. In *ikebana*, the heavens are the highest branch, man the middle branch, the earth the lower branch. If three stones are used, the highest will be the heavens, a horizontal stone will be man, a flat stone the earth. Heavens signify light, earth shadow. Man is situated between light and darkness.

Sōtō
Japanese *Zen* sect founded by Dōgen (1243).

Suisei-mushi
Expresses the fact of being born, living and dying in a waking dream, which is the lot of the great majority of men. As opposed to the idea of man, a part of the Great Whole.

Suki
Expresses the sense of openness, the sense of an empty space (*suki-ku*), designates a particular taste shown in the disposition of objects. In martial arts, *suki* designates the cerebral void, the moment of inattention.

Sukima

Void, absence of thought, of action, 'dead time'.

Sukiya

The architecture of the tea mansion, where the *chanoyu* tea ceremony is practised.

Sutemi

'Sacrifice': word employed in *jūdō* and in all the *budō*, expresses the idea of throwing the body, of throwing life as one enters death, with an absolute decisiveness and spirit of sacrifice. Without a *sutemi*, or absolute movement of self-abandonment in attack, the frontier of the ego brings about defeat.

Tachi (or Dachi)

Long ceremonial sword. Standing position.

Tachi-Oyogi

Special martial swimming stoke or 'swimming standing up', making it possible to get across a river while fully armed.

T'ai-chi

Chinese word for the supreme ultimate. The highest summit.

T'ai-chi-Ch'uan

Chinese martial art, commonly called 'shadow boxing' composing a system of body movements designed to achieve physical, mental, emotional and spiritual harmony.

Tama

Signifies the *anima*, the soul.

According to Shinto, the human soul is composed of four elements The *ara- (mi) tama*, or faculty generating its own ideas; the *nigi- (mi) tama*, or faculty of consolidating and organizing the material world; *saki- (mi) tama*, or faculty of analyzing, separating and differentiating the world into its constitutive elements; *kushi- (mi) tama*, or faculty of penetrating and unifying in a centre the worlds of matter and mind.

The supreme realization of man is the faculty of unifying the multiple in the one.

The human soul is symbolized in *Shinto* by a helical spiral that expresses universality being absorbed into the one.

Tanden

According to the Buddhist conception, the *tanden* is the centre of man, situated about 2cm below the navel, (on representations of the Buddha it is often indicated by a lotus). Here is the origin of all spiritual and corporal strength, and the basic exercise consists in concentrating on the exact tension of the abdominal muscles. The spiritual axis of man and his centre of gravity pass through the *tanden*. It is the original source of 'vital' strength. 'The whole art of mastering the *tanden*', says a Japanese master, Sajō Tsuji, 'resides in this: after having liberated all the forces spread throughout the body, we must direct and unite them in the *tanden*; this art has always been taught in *budō* (knightly way), *geidō* (artistic way) and *sadō* (art of 'posture').' This point of the belly is also called *seika tanden*, an expression coming from Chinese Taoism: it signifies 'river of cinnabar'. In Japanese it is also called *kikai*, ocean of *ki*. (See the words *Hara* and *Ki*.)

Tao
Supreme essence of existence, fundamental concept of Taoism. Also Dao.

Taoism
The philosophy of *Tao*. Chinese religion founded according to tradition by Lao-Tsu in the sixth century BC. Lao-Tsu is thought to have been the author of the *Tao-te-Ching*, the principal sacred work of *Taoism*. *Tao* is a word that defies all attempt at exact definition. It signifies 'way', 'road', 'path' and expresses a sense of unity with the whole of Creation.

Tatami
Carpet made out of compressed straw matting which the Japanese use both in rooms for martial-arts training, and for sleeping on.

Tanabata
Festival of the stars, in June. Celebrates the annual meeting of Altair and Vega on the Milky Way (the spinner and her divine lover). Celebration of Chinese origin. From arches over the streets are hung bamboos decorated with lanterns and paper flames, with packets of sweets. Little girls are given presents of embroidery thread, silk, etc.

Utsuroi
Expression of what is ephemeral, idea of the time that passes, reflection. Used to describe the gossamer colours of scattered flowers. A quivering springs out of the darkness and touches the surface of water or earth. Attitude that seeks to define space in terms of vibration.

Wa (peace)
Unique term in Japanese to designate the two concepts of 'harmony' and 'communion': there is perhaps no word that better illustrates the essence of Nippon civilization.

Wabi
Expresses essential poverty and simplicity. Whence the practice of constructing an object of great beauty, indeed something very delicate, out of the simplest and cheapest materials. Spirit that results from the tea ceremony: cha-no-yu. Attitude expressing a profound respect towards the humblest things in nature. The traditional Japanese wooden house expresses the concept of *wabi*.

Wakaru
Dividing. Cutting in two.

Waza
Technique, art.

Yamato
Great peace or harmony. Original name for Japan, region of Nara. The country of the Great Peace. See **Wa**.

Yabusame
Archery on horseback, today a *Shinto* ceremony.

Yama
Mountain. Ethics, inner purification.

Yari
Lance.

Yin-Yang
The Chinese word *Yin* represents all that is negative or passive, inert, soft, material, heavy, dark, feminine. *Yang* all that is positive, active, expansive, moving, hard, light, luminous, masculine. *Yin* undergoes movement, *Yang* executes it. Nothing is entirely *Yang* or entirely *Yin*. *Yin* engenders *Yang*, *Yang* engenders *Yin*.

Yō
Japanese word for Yang. Active mental state, opposed to the passive mental state *in* (analogous to Chinese *yang* and *yin*).

Yokozuna
Thick cord that *sumō* champions wear around their waist for festivals or ceremonies. The *Yokozuna* is a symbol of dignity and moral integrity, and only the very greatest of champions may wear it. By extension,

Yokozuna means a great champion.

Yomi

The obscurity of darkness which is lit intermittently. In the nō theatre or in traditional dance, the actors or dancers emerge from total darkness to the glow of a feeble light.

Zanshin

Reflection. Eighth and last position in archery. Expresses, in archery, the idea that the shot continues, or the keeping going of the shot.

Zazen

Seated meditation in Zen.

Zen

Discipline that leads to self-realization. Derived from the Chinese Ch'an (q.v.) which is itself a linguistic corruption of the sanskrit word *dhyāna*, which means meditation.

INDEX

Of further interest

THE MASTER,
THE MONKS, AND I

In the spring of 1963 the German actress Gerta Ital boarded a plane at Frankfurt to fly to Japan in search of a Zen Master. It was a journey into the unknown with no guarantee of success, and it was to cost her everything.

In due course she became a disciple of Rôshi Mumon Yamada, the direct successor of Hakuin and one of the most revered of all living Zen Masters. In accepting her, Rôshi Mumon broke with the traditions of Zen in a dramatic and radical way and sparked off a storm of protest both inside and outside the monastery.

Gerta Ital did not go to Japan to observe or study Zen: she went to *live* it. Her compelling and often moving account describes the path of Zen as it is followed daily by ordinary human beings, with all their failings. In her search for enlightenment Ms Ital encountered intrigue and jealousy side by side with extreme physical hardship, debilitating despair, and moments of blissful transcendence.

Though she never abandoned her Christianity, Gerta Ital's pilgrimage took her beyond all religions and traditions. Zen, the path of paradox, taught her — as it teaches us — one thing: experience what *is*, and leave everything else behind you — including Zen.